Jerusalem:
Where Empires Die

by
LESTER SUMRALL

THOMAS NELSON PUBLISHERS
Nashville • Camden • New York

Published in Nashville, Tennessee, by Thomas Nelson,
Inc. and distributed in Canada by Lawson Falle, Ltd.,
Cambridge, Ontario.

Printed in the United States of America.

Library of Congress Cataloging in Publication Data

Sumrall, Lester Frank, 1913-
  Jerusalem, where empirs die.

  1. Bible—Prophecies—Jerusalem. 2. Jerusalem in the
Bible. 3. Jerusalem—History. I. Title.
BS649.J38S85 1984   231.7'45   84-4908
ISBN 0-8407-5865-0

Jerusalem:
Where Empires Die

Contents

Introduction

"Will America die at Jerusalem?" In this book I am going to reveal a lesson of immense importance, a crucial fact of history that God would have us understand, because it will play a decisive role in the future of the United States.

As we look over the pages of history, we see a remarkable thing. Every empire that has won control over the known world of its time has been drawn irresistibly and mysteriously to Jerusalem. The leaders of these empires have felt a compulsion to go to Jerusalem and conquer it, enslaving its people. Those leaders probably did not realize the forces at work behind their decisions to go to Jerusalem; but God did, Satan did, and God wants us to be aware as well.

The fact is that Jerusalem has been a spiritual battleground down through the ages. Jerusalem is a city loved by God and chosen by Him to be His earthly dwelling place, as well as the capital of His chosen people, Israel. Because God loves the city and its citizens so much, Satan hates it passionately and has inspired those world emperors to march against it.

God has not loved and chosen Jerusalem only to neglect its welfare. And this is the lesson God would have us learn: The decision to move against Jerusalem has been the beginning of the end for every one of those world empires. From that point in time, those nations have been judged by God and doomed to destruction.

As we look at Jerusalem with that key theme in mind, we will want to look at the story of the conquests of Jerusalem by those pagan empires, and we will see how such world powers came to their ends. To fully appreciate the city and everything God would have us know about it, we will also look at such things as the city's part in the life of Christ and how it came to be the capital of the modern state of Israel. We will then look at the city in the light of biblical prophecy to see how, in the end times, it will play a crucial role in the downfall of the last two empires that will oppose God.

We will conclude this book by applying what we have learned to the United States today. Please read that chapter very carefully and prayerfully.

God loves Jerusalem very much, and so do I. My love for the city has been strengthened by the more than fifty trips I have made to it, alone and at the head of tour groups. Each time I go, as I walk the streets and meditate and pray, my love and appreciation for the city grows.

I love Jerusalem so much that on one occasion I moved my family to the city and lived there for almost seven months. We went there to try to better understand its people. And during the course of our stay, the Sinai War of 1956 took place. I was also in the city, leading a group of tourists, for the entirety of the Yom Kippur War in 1973. I have seen the city in both good times and bad.

This book is written to clarify a crucial fact of history, and to warn America of the need to be very careful in relations with Israel. But it is also written out of my great love for Jerusalem; and it is my prayer for you as you read that you will not only learn and be warned, but also will grow to know and love the city as I have, and thereby understand and love more than ever before the One who owns Jerusalem.

Jerusalem:
Where Empires Die

1

Jerusalem: The Mystic City

Jerusalem is a city unlike any other in the world, of special, unique importance to God. The things He has said about her, indicating how He regards her, He has said about no other city. Jerusalem has already played a larger role in the unfolding of God's plan for the ages than any other metropolis, and she will continue to do so. All this reflects and is a part of the special regard God has for the city.

In this chapter we want to look at what the Bible tells us about the unique relationship God has with Jerusalem. It is mentioned more often in the Bible than any other city—indeed, many of the historical events recorded in the Bible took place there. That is no accident or coincidence; it was not just David who chose Jerusalem as the capital city of Israel and the site of God's temple. God Himself set apart the city for His purposes. Let's look at some of the aspects of God's unique relationship with the city.

The Beloved City

The Bible tells us first that *God loves the city of Jerusalem in a special way*. We may believe with certainty that God loves the people in every city, but His regard for Jerusalem is unique. No other city is lauded in the Bible in the way that Jerusalem is.

Psalm 87:2 tells us, "The LORD loves the gates of Zion/ More than all the dwellings of Jacob." Zion is literally one of the hills on which Jerusalem is built, but the name is used more generally as a synonym for Jerusalem. So this verse says that of all the places in God's Holy Land, Jerusalem, the land He gave to Abraham and his descendants—His chosen people—is the one He loves most.

Similarly, Psalm 78:68 says that God "chose the tribe of Judah,/ Mount Zion which He loved." Here again, of all the cities of Israel, Jerusalem is singled out as the object of God's special affection. She is precious to Him, more precious than any other city.

For further evidence of God's love for Jerusalem, consider Jesus' lamentation over the city in Luke 13:34. Jesus was on His way to Jerusalem and had just been warned that it would be dangerous for Him to go there, because King Herod wanted to kill Him. How did He react? Did He become angry or take offense? No. He said, "O Jerusalem, Jerusalem, the one who kills the prophets and stones those who are sent to her! How often I wanted to gather your children together, as a hen gathers her brood under her wings, but you were not willing!"

Here He was speaking as the incarnate God, expressing His great love for the city, saying He longed to draw her people to Himself in arms of love. Only the rebelliousness of the people kept them from enjoying that tender, protective love of God.

Why does God love Jerusalem so much, especially when her people have been so rebellious against Him? We cannot know for sure. Why does He love the Jewish people in a special way? Why does He love you and me? Jerusalem is a beautiful city, the capital city of the land He set aside for His chosen people. Those facts tell us a little of why He should love her in a special way, but they do not really explain why He should necessarily love her above all other cities. As with the question of why He loves us, we must conclude that it is a matter of God's sovereign will, and simply thank Him and praise Him for it.

The Chosen City

In accord with God's unique love for Jerusalem, the Bible describes Jerusalem as *God's chosen city*. Psalm 132:13 says, "For the LORD has chosen Zion." Zechariah 3:2 speaks of "the LORD who has chosen Jerusalem." In 2 Chronicles 6:6 God tells us, "I have chosen Jerusalem, that My name may be there." And Isaiah 14:32 puts the same thought in slightly different form when it says, "the LORD has founded Zion."

Here again we see God's unique regard for the city. She is His chosen city, set apart for Him. The Bible says nothing like this of Damascus, Tyre, Babylon, Athens, Rome, or any other city. Of all the world's cities, Jerusalem is the one God has specially chosen.

God's Dwelling Place

For what purpose has God chosen Jerusalem for Himself? There are several scriptural passages that give us an idea. For example, Psalm 132:13-14 reads, "For the LORD has chosen Zion;/ He has desired it for His habitation:/ 'This is My resting place forever;/ Here I will dwell, for I have desired it.' " We get a similar picture from Psalm 76:2: "In Salem [Jerusalem] also is His tabernacle,/ And His dwelling place in Zion."

We see from these passages that God chose to dwell on earth in Jerusalem—specifically, in the Temple. You will remember that when Israel completed the tabernacle in the wilderness and dedicated it, a cloud covered it and the glory of the Lord filled it (see Ex. 40:34-35). God also gave Israel, by command, the Ark of the Covenant to be placed in the tabernacle's Holy of Holies, and there He promised to meet with them and reveal His will to them (see Ex. 25:22).

When Jerusalem became established as Israel's capital and God allowed Solomon to build a permanent temple, the Ark was moved there, and with it came the glorious cloud signifying God's presence in the Shekinah glory.

> And it came to pass, when the priests came out of the holy place, that the cloud filled the house of the LORD, so that the priests could not continue ministering because of the cloud; for the glory of the LORD filled the house of the LORD (1 Kin. 8:10-11).

Then Jerusalem was the dwelling place of God on earth.

You will also recall, however, that because of Israel's unfaithfulness in continual rebellion and idolatry, the glory of God—His abiding presence—departed from the Temple, as recorded in Ezekiel's vision (see Ezek. 10:18-19). Today, of course, the Jewish Temple does not stand, and God does not dwell there in the same sense in which He did in the times of Moses and David.

But we also know from Scripture that the day will come when the glory of the Lord will be restored to Jerusalem. Psalm 48:8 tells us, "God will establish it forever." Ezekiel also foresaw in a vision that God would return there to dwell forever (see Ezek. 43:4-9). And in the New Jerusalem seen by John in his vision, there won't even be a need for a temple, for the Lord God Almighty and the Lamb will be its temple (see Rev. 21:22).

So we see that God has chosen Jerusalem to be His earthly abode. Israel forfeited the privilege of His continual presence in the Temple many years ago, but there is coming a time when His glorious presence will return. And one day, those of us who are God's children through faith in the finished work of Jesus Christ will dwell with Him in a New Jerusalem whose builder and maker is God, and whose light is His glory.

The Blessed City

We have seen that God loves Jerusalem and chose her to be His dwelling place. Realizing that, it is not surprising that *God has promised to bless and protect her*. In Psalm 46:5, the psalmist declared of Jerusalem, "God is in the midst of her,/ she shall not be moved; God shall help her,/ just at the break of dawn."

This love for and desire to help and protect Jerusalem is like the love of a father for his children, constant and strong, even when circumstances might tend to cast doubt on that love. As we will see in the next chapter, Jerusalem has suffered through numerous calamitous events. Seeing such things, we may be tempted to ask, "If God loves and wants to protect Jerusalem, why did He allow that?" But just as a father disciplines the children he loves, and just as he sometimes allows them to suffer the painful consequences of their rebellious decisions, knowing that is the only way they will ever learn, so we may assume God has been dealing with Jerusalem down through history.

As a father, I know it is not easy to keep silent and watch a child go down a path that is certain to lead to pain of some kind. Surely God the Father's heart has been broken many times as He watched the people of His chosen city turn their backs on Him to pursue sinful lifestyles. I, like all fathers, know in some small measure how He has felt. And even though you try to watch over them and be there afterward to comfort them in their hurt, you have to let them learn from their mistakes. Thus God has dealt with the willful rebelliousness of the inhabitants of Jerusalem.

This willingness of God to discipline Jerusalem and let her reap the consequences of her sinful sowing has been interpreted by many people to mean He no longer cares about Jerusalem, and people are, therefore, free to do what they will to her. Nothing is further from the truth, and we may be sure God is watching over Jerusalem and keeping accounts.

We see a beautiful illustration of this concern of God for Jerusalem and reckoning against her persecutors in the first chapter of Zechariah. When Zechariah wrote the prophecy God gave him, most of the people of Jerusalem had been taken captive to Babylon. Some, however, had been allowed by the Persian king Cyrus and his successor, Darius, to return to Jerusalem and rebuild the Temple.

In his vision in chapter 1, Zechariah sees a conversation between the Lord and an angel. He hears the angel ask God in verse 12, "O LORD of hosts, how long will You not have mercy on Jerusalem and on the cities of Judah, against which You were angry these seventy years?" After God answered the angel (which Zechariah either didn't hear or didn't record), the angel said to Zechariah on God's behalf:

"Thus says the LORD of hosts: 'I am zealous for Jerusalem/ And for Zion with a great zeal. I am exceedingly angry with the nations at ease; For I was a little angry,/ And they helped—but with evil intent' " (vv. 14–15).

There we see the passion of God for Jerusalem, and clear evidence that God does indeed watch over the city and note what is done to her. He said, in effect, "This city is very precious to Me. I am zealous for her. Those who hurt her, hurt Me. And although I allowed the Babylonians to capture Jerusalem as a way of disciplining her, they went too far by trying to annihilate her. This affront to My beloved city is an affront to Me, and I will not overlook it."

So it has ever been, and so it will always be. Those who harm Jerusalem will not escape the notice of God. And what will befall those who persecute God's city? We get a hint in Psalm 129:5: "Let all those who hate Zion/ Be put to shame and turned back." This imprecation from the psalmist suggests that in some way there will be dire consequences for those who hate and harm Jerusalem.

In contrast to that curse upon those who hate Jerusalem, the psalmist David offered this blessing to those who love her: "Pray for the peace of Jerusalem: 'May they prosper who love you' " (Ps. 122:6). This is the reverse side of the issue, the good promised to those who love the city God loves.

The Exalted City

Corresponding to the special place Jerusalem has in the heart of God, the Bible gives her many exalted names that identify her and express God's regard for her. These are further evidence for the city's unique relationship with the Lord.

In Psalm 46:4, for example, Jerusalem is called "the city of God." It is "the city of our God" in several places (Ps. 48:1,8). Psalm 87:3 adds, "Glorious things are spoken of you, O city of God!"

In a similar vein, the city is elsewhere identified as "the city of the great King" (Ps. 48:2). Jesus also gave it this name in Matthew 5:35. Jerusalem is "the city of the LORD of hosts" (Ps. 48:8). We are given a beautiful image of God's love for the city in Psalm 48:1, where it is described as "In His holy mountain."

The Bible also gives us warm descriptive phrases that show how both God and men admire and love the city. The psalmist Asaph, for example, called Jerusalem "the perfection of beauty" (Ps. 50:2). Another psalmist expressed the same sentiment in saying the city is "beautiful in elevation" (Ps. 48:2), an altogether lovely city. In the same verse he described Jerusalem as "the joy of the whole earth."

I feel certain that these exalting names given to Jerusalem by the psalmists come straight from the heart of God, by His inspiration. They reflect His overwhelming love for the city, a love unique to Jerusalem. At the same time, they no doubt reveal as well the love of the human writers who penned them.

If God loves Jerusalem above all other cities, chose her for His earthly dwelling place in the Shekinah glory, and keeps a close watch over her, as we have seen in these passages of Scripture, it should not surprise us in the least that Satan despises the city passionately and has tried throughout history to reduce it to rubble permanently. As we look at the story of the city from ancient times forward, and as we see how the world's great empires have been drawn irresistibly to her in an attempt to subjugate her, we should keep in mind the verses we have just studied. They explain why the abuse of Jerusalem has been the beginning of the end for those empires, why empires die at Jerusalem.

2

Jerusalem: Where Empires Die

We have seen the biblical witness to God's special regard for and promise to protect Jerusalem. A former mayor of the city, the last Arab mayor, acknowledged God's watching over it when he said as he fled in front of the oncoming Israeli army, "Jerusalem is a golden bowl full of vipers. They that put their hand in the bowl, die." That truly is the lesson of history, as we will see in this chapter as we look at the story of the city, with a special emphasis on major world empires of the past and their deaths at Jerusalem.

In the Beginning

We do not know for certain when a city was first built on the site of Jerusalem. Its origin is lost in antiquity. The Bible's first mention of the city states its reality simply, without explanation.

That initial biblical reference to Jerusalem comes in Genesis 14:18, where we are also introduced to the mysterious Melchizedek, its king, who was also a priest of God. At that time the city was known as Salem. We are not told anything more about the city at that point.

The city was next known as Jebus, so named after the people who inhabited it, the Jebusites. When Israel first entered Canaan under Joshua's leadership at the end of the Exodus, the city was assigned to the tribe of Benjamin (see Josh. 18:28).

That assignment only meant, however, that Jebus was in the territory allotted to Benjamin. It remained for the Israelites to capture the city and inhabit it. But they were unable to do so initially, as we read in Judges 1:21: "But the children of Benjamin did not drive out the Jebusites who inhabited Jerusalem to this day [i.e., the day when Judges 1 was written]."

The city of Jebus was obviously not easy to capture, as it was built on a hill and fortified, making it relatively simple to defend. As far as we know, the Jebusites kept control of the city for approximately four hundred years before the Israelites were finally able to capture it.

The Israelite City

Israel's King David finally conquered the city. And even when he went to take it, it was still a formidable stronghold. In fact, the Jebusites were so confident David could not defeat them that they said, " 'You shall not come in here; but the blind and the lame will repel you' " (2 Sam. 5:6). In other words, they thought their fortifications were so strong that the blind and the lame could easily defend the city against David and his men.

David, however, found a way into the city through its water shaft ("gutter" in KJV; see 2 Sam. 5:8) and captured it. He took up residence in the city, called it the City of David, and began to build it up (see 2 Sam. 5:9). It became his, and Israel's, capital city.

Any person at all familiar with the psalms knows that David was a devout follower and ardent lover of God. It is not surprising, therefore, that one day—undoubtedly after giving the matter a great deal of thought—David said to Nathan the prophet as he sat in his house, " 'See now, I dwell in a house of cedar, but the ark of the covenant of the LORD is under tent curtains' " (1 Chr. 17:1).

Then Nathan replied to David, " 'Do all that is in your heart, for God is with you' " (1 Chr. 17:2). David was thinking it wasn't right for him to have a fine, permanent house while God's dwelling was still the tent of a nomadic people. And Nathan told David to go ahead with his desire to build a temple.

Nathan spoke too soon, however, as God did not want David to build His temple (see 1 Chr. 17:3–4). David explained God's reasoning to his son Solomon:

> "The word of the LORD came to me, saying, 'You have shed much blood and have made great wars; you shall not build a house for My name, because you have shed much blood on the earth in My sight' " (1 Chr. 22:8).

David was a great warrior, a man of violence, and God did not want such a man to be the one to build His earthly house, despite David's devotion.

God did honor David's desire to build a temple, however, as He explained to David:

> " 'Behold, a son shall be born to you, who shall be a man of rest; and I will give him rest from all his enemies all around...I will give peace and quietness to Israel in his days. He shall build a house for My name' " (1 Chr. 22:9–10).

That son of David was Solomon, of course, and the last few verses I have quoted come from David's charge to Solomon to build the Temple.

Even though David could not build the Temple, he did bring the Ark of the Covenant into Jerusalem (see 2 Sam. 6:12-17), and he made many of the preparations for the construction of the Temple (see 1 Chr. 22:1-5,14-19). He had stones hewn for its foundation, and he collected brass, cedar wood, gold, silver, iron for nails, and skillful men to work with all these materials.

Solomon did build God's Temple, and under Solomon the kingdom of Israel enjoyed its greatest power and prosperity. The reason for that success, in my opinion, was the understanding of, and humility before, God that Solomon revealed as he was dedicating the newly completed Temple. In his prayer to the Lord on that occasion, he said, " 'But will God indeed dwell on the earth? behold, the heaven and heaven of heavens cannot contain thee; how much less this house which I have built?' " (1 Kin. 8:27 KJV).

Solomon was very much aware at that point in his life of the greatness and majesty of God, and he knew the Temple could not really hold God; He dwelt there in the Shekinah glory only as an expression of His special concern for Israel.

Solomon built more than just the Temple. Although he put seven years into building the Temple, he spent thirteen years building a magnificent palace for himself in Jerusalem. And in his palace he put a great throne of ivory overlaid with the best gold (see 1 Kin. 10:18-20). He also built cities for storage and to house his chariots and horsemen (see 1 Kin. 9:17-19), and he built a navy to carry on trade by sea with other nations (see 1 Kin. 9:26-28).

At the height of Solomon's reign, he had made Jerusalem into a city without peer in the world of his day—strongly fortified, secure, boasting the most beautiful architecture, and filled with all the finest of the nation's goods, including horses and other animals, wood, clothing, spices, armor, and chariots. He was the earth's richest and greatest king, and Jerusalem was its richest and greatest city (see 1 Kin. 10:21-29).

Unfortunately, later in Solomon's life he lost the proper perspective concerning God and married many heathen wives. When he did that, he also built places of worship for their pagan gods. The result was a severe spiritual decline in Israel, and after Solomon's death the kingdom was split (approximately 925 B.C.). Many of the kings of Judah and all the kings of Israel thereafter were far more wicked than Solomon.

Jerusalem continued to be a capital city, but only of the smaller kingdom of Judah. Jerusalem had been capital of a united Israel for only approximately eighty years.

Jerusalem's Troubles Begin

The division of Solomon's realm into the separate kingdoms of Israel and Judah was more than merely political. The split began in animosity, and the antagonism between the two continued down through the years, with a virtual state of war permanently in effect.

This constant state of tension between the northern kingdom of Israel and the southern kingdom of Judah, which was loyal to the descendants of David, reached a climax in approximately 800 B.C. At that point, the armies of the two kingdoms met in battle at Beth Shemesh in the land of Judah, about fifteen miles west of Jerusalem. Judah under King Amaziah was defeated by Israel under King Jehoash. Having won the battle, Jehoash went to Jerusalem, broke down part of the city wall, sacked the Temple, took hostages, and returned to his capital of Samaria (see 2 Kin. 14:11–14).

Israel at Jerusalem

King Jehoash should have known better than to abuse God's Holy City. After all, he had access to the testimonies of David concerning God's love for Jerusalem, as well as those of the prophets Elijah, Elisha, and Obadiah. By ignoring God's devotion to the city, however, Jehoash set his nation on a course to disaster.

Israel's downfall provides us with our first example of how God has used one world power to punish another that had tangled with Jerusalem. Just seventy-five years after Jehoash's desecration of Jerusalem (a relatively brief time in the context of history), the mighty Assyrian Empire came up against Israel. The Assyrians besieged Samaria for three years, finally conquering it and sending its people into exile (see 2 Kin. 17:5–6). Thus did the people of Israel suffer for their idolatrous rejection of God and their defiling of His city.

Assyria Dies at Jerusalem

Having defeated Israel, Assyria determined to conquer Judah as well. Inspired by Satan, King Sennacherib moved against the southern kingdom in approximately 700 B.C. The Assyrians first captured the "fortified cities" of Judah (2 Kin. 18:13), and then they marched on Jerusalem. Sennacherib sent men to within shouting distance of Jerusalem's walls to try to discourage the people with the message that their defeat was inevitable and their God would be of no help to them.

We can all take a lesson in how to respond to adverse circumstances from Judah's King Hezekiah. When he heard how the Assyrians and their henchmen were blaspheming God—they even sent him a letter saying he shouldn't trust the Lord—he went to the Lord in prayer and asked Him to save the city. God heard Hezekiah's prayer, and through the prophet Isaiah He sent this message:

> "Therefore thus says the LORD concerning the king of Assyria:
> 'He shall not come into this city,
> Nor shoot an arrow there,
> Nor come before it with shield,
> Nor build a siege mound against it. . . .
> For I will defend this city, to save it
> For My own sake,
> and for My servant David's sake' " (2 Kin. 19:32,34).

God then did a miracle in defense of Jerusalem.

> And it came to pass on a certain night that the angel of the LORD went out, and killed in the camp of the Assyrians one hundred and eighty-five thousand; and when people arose early in the morning, there were the corpses—all dead. So Sennacherib king of Assyria departed and went away, returned home and remained at Nineveh (2 Kin. 19:35–36).

End of siege! Now that's an answer to prayer!

The destruction of Assyria's army was not the end of God's judgment against Sennacherib and his nation, however. For after the king's return to his capital, "as he was worshiping in the temple of Nisroch his god, . . . his sons

Adrammelech and Sharezer struck him down with the sword; and they escaped into the land of Ararat" (2 Kin. 19:37).

The downfall of the mighty Assyrian Empire came just seventy-five years after its ill-fated assault on Jerusalem. Sennacherib's arrogance in the face of God's avowed love for the city was inexcusable. Having taken captive the northern kingdom of Israel, he had the testimony of devout Israelites living in his land, but he chose to ignore it. God had been faithful to provide a witness, to give Assyria a clear choice between right and wrong, and it had deliberately chosen to challenge God.

The instrument of God's judgment against Assyria was the next world empire, Babylon. The might of Assyria was crushed in 625 B.C. by the Babylonians under Nabopolassar, with help from the Medes.

Babylon Dies at Jerusalem

Once again, a world empire set its sights on the conquest of Jerusalem, then ruled by Jehoiakim. Not long after defeating Assyria, Nebuchadnezzar, king of Babylon, defeated Egypt at the Battle of Carchemish in 605 B.C. and then turned toward Jerusalem. He besieged and captured the city, spilling much blood in the process, and took some of the precious vessels from the Temple. He also took a number of captives, including the young Daniel (see 2 Kin. 24:1; Dan. 1:1–6).

Jehoiakim died and was replaced by his son Jehoiachin. Shortly after Jehoiachin assumed the throne, Nebuchadnezzar again came and besieged the city, and Jehoiachin surrendered to him (see 2 Kin. 24:10–12). Once again the Temple and palace were plundered of all valuables, and more people were taken into exile in Babylon (see 2 Kin. 24:13–16).

Nebuchadnezzar then installed Zedekiah as king of Judah in place of Jehoiachin, whom he had taken into exile. Just a few years later, in 588 B.C., Zedekiah rebelled against Babylon. So once again, Nebuchadnezzar brought his army and besieged Jerusalem. The siege lasted eighteen months, and the people of Jerusalem, cut off from the world outside, ran out of food. Then finally the Babylonians broke into the city and captured it.

King Zedekiah and his army fled, but they were overtaken and captured on the plains of Jericho, east of the city. Zedekiah was led before Nebuchadnezzar, who judged him for his rebellion. As his punishment, Zedekiah was forced to watch the slaughter of his sons, and then his eyes were put out and he was taken to Babylon in fetters.

Having done that, Nebuchadnezzar sent the captain of his guard to Jerusalem to burn down the city, tear down its walls, and take all but the poorest people captive into Babylon. The city, including the Temple, was in ruins, and most of its inhabitants who had not been killed were in exile (see 2 Kin. 24:17–25:12). (Another group of people had fled to Egypt, taking with them, despite his protests, the prophet Jeremiah.) The proud city of David and Solomon was a nearly deserted pile of rubble, and the peace those great kings had brought was a distant memory.

After that last, utter destruction of Jerusalem, God's judgment against Babylon was not long in coming. A short forty-nine years later, on a fateful night in 539 B.C., God called Babylon to account for its mistreatment of Jerusalem.

On that night the Babylonian king Belshazzar made a great feast for a thousand of his nobles, and everyone at the feast was drinking wine (we can safely infer they were probably drinking to the point of drunkenness). Then, in a decision born of arrogance and complete lack of respect for the God of Israel, Belshazzar ordered that the gold and silver vessels his predecessor Nebuchadnezzar had taken from the Temple in Jerusalem be brought in so he and his guests could drink from them (see Dan. 5:1-2). The vessels were brought and used in idolatrous revelry: "The king and his lords, his wives, and his concubines drank from them. They drank wine, and praised the gods of gold and silver, bronze and iron, wood and stone" (Dan. 5:3-4).

To use the Temple vessels, which had been consecrated for the worship of God, in such a way was a direct affront to Him. We read next:

> In the same hour the fingers of a man's hand appeared and wrote opposite the lampstand on the plaster of the wall of the king's palace; and the king saw the part of the hand that wrote. Then the king's countenance was changed, and his thoughts troubled him, so that the joints of his hips were loosened and his knees knocked against each other (Dan. 5:5-6).

Picture the scene in your mind if you can. The king was so scared that his knees were literally knocking together.

Belshazzar called in all his astrologers and soothsayers to tell him what the writing said, but none of them could decipher it. The queen then reminded the king of the wisdom and interpretive ability of the prophet Daniel. Daniel was called in, and he told Belshazzar that because he had not been humble but instead had exalted himself against the Lord of heaven, God had judged Babylon and found it guilty. Therefore, the kingdom of Babylon was to be given to the Persians (see Dan. 5:7-28).

That very night, the Persians diverted the Euphrates River

that normally flowed through Babylon, allowing them to enter the city by the riverbed. They found the king and the people in their drunken festival, and "that very night Belshazzar, king of the Chaldeans, was slain" (Dan. 5:30). The Babylonian Empire was no more.

We should note again that Babylon was fully guilty before God in its abuse of Jerusalem. God had been faithful to provide a witness to His laws, this time in the very highest circles of government, in the person of Daniel. So Babylon was without excuse when it attacked the city, and without defense when God condemned it.

Persia and Greece

The conqueror of Babylon was Cyrus the Great, the founder of the Persian Empire. Compared to previous rulers, the Persians were relatively lenient toward Jerusalem and the Jews. The year after defeating Babylon, Cyrus the Great issued an edict emancipating the Jews, and a year later 42,360 Jews with 7,337 servants returned to Jerusalem to rebuild the Temple. Their leader was Zerubbabel, a prince of the house of David (see Ezra 2:64-65; 3:8).

The city was still lying in ruins as a result of the Babylonian wars, and the emigrants despaired of their rebuilding task. We can sympathize when we remember it took Solomon, with his great wealth and supply of manpower, seven years to build it in the first place. As so often happens when a job looks impossible, the people assigned to it became apathetic. They were encouraged in their work, however, by the prophets Haggai and Zechariah, and you can read of their roles in the Old Testament books bearing their names.

The reconstruction continued, and the second Temple was

completed in 516 B.C., a work of approximately twenty years. In Jewish tradition, that date is regarded as the true end of the seventy-year-long Babylonian exile. The Temple was reconsecrated in 515 B.C.

When we look at the fate of the Temple over the course of the years, keep in mind its significance to the Jews. I cannot stress this enough. It was the *one* Temple, the only place where sacrifices could be made to the Lord, the only dwelling place of God on earth. When the Jews were forced to leave their land—and they *never* left it voluntarily—they developed the synagogue system of worship still in use today; but always the dream was to rebuild the Temple in Jerusalem, for there could be no substitute for it.

After the Temple had been rebuilt under the leadership of Zerubbabel, the task of rebuilding the rest of the city continued, but slowly. In 445 B.C., Nehemiah, cupbearer to the Persian king Artaxerxes, heard that the walls of the city were still in a shambles and received permission from the king to go to Jerusalem and reconstruct them. Nehemiah proved to be an eminently capable leader, as you will see when you read his book in the Bible, and the city's walls were completed in just fifty-two days under his direction. He was aided by the spiritual leadership of the prophet Ezra.

As time went on, more and more Jews returned to Judah and Jerusalem and worked at rebuilding other parts of the city.

In 330 B.C., Greece defeated Persia under the leadership of its legendary ruler, Alexander the Great. Jerusalem was once again under a new master. The reign of Greece was brief, however, because when Alexander died seven years later at age thirty-three, his kingdom was divided; and Judea was given to Ptolemy of Egypt. A succession of Egyptian kings (known as Ptolemies) continued in authority over Jerusalem for many years, until 198 B.C., when yet another power fought for and won control of Judea.

Abomination and Revolt

In that year, the Seleucid Empire (Syria) under its king, Antiochus III ("the Great"), took Judea from Egypt. Meanwhile, during the years of the Greek, Egyptian, and then Syrian rule, the influence of Greek culture, religion, and philosophy continued to grow, a process known as Hellenization. (Its influence was still strong in New Testament times, as witnessed by the fact that the New Testament was originally written in Greek, the universal language of the known world.)

The Jewish upper classes were becoming Hellenized, but the promoters of the movement were important, so they tried to force a cultural revolution on the people with the support of the next Seleucid king, Antiochus IV (Antiochus Epiphanes). He took that goal to the extreme, outlawing the Jewish religion, forbidding circumcision and observance of the Sabbath, burning holy Scriptures, and desecrating the Temple in 167 B.C. by sacrificing a pig on its altar. He then made the Temple into a shrine to Zeus. The idea was to replace Judaism with Hellenism in all its aspects, including the worship of Greek gods.

As has been noted before by many commentators, Antiochus IV was truly a predecessor of the Antichrist who will appear in the last days. Antiochus's desire to promote Hellenism was only a small part of the reason for his persecution of the Jews. He was a violent, evil man who hated God, His people, and His beloved city.

33

The abominations of Antiochus IV sparked a God-in-spired revolt on the part of the Jewish people against their Syrian ruler. It was led by Mattathias—a priest—and his sons Jonathan and Simon—the brothers of Judas Macca-baeus. After a bitter military struggle with bloodshed, the Maccabees prevailed over Syria and captured Jerusalem in 165 B.C. The Temple was reconsecrated in 164 B.C., allow-ing Jewish worship there to begin again.

Simon of the Maccabees then established the Macca-baean, otherwise known as the Hasmonaean, dynasty in Je-rusalem, and the Jews had their own king for one hundred years.

During that time, the Sadducees and the Pharisees came into being as political parties. They differed in religious doctrine as well as in political theory (e.g., see Acts 23:6–8), and we see much of them in the life of Jesus Christ as they opposed Him and His work.

In those years the Hasmonaeans also established the San-hedrin, a council of state composed of seventy-one Jewish leaders and sages, which was the supreme authority for civil and religious legal decisions in the capital city of Jerusalem. It was to this council that Jesus was first taken for trial after His arrest (see Matt. 26:57, where the council is identified as "the scribes and the elders").

The Hasmonaean dynasty was also the period of the be-ginning of monastic, communal brotherhoods such as the Essenes, who believed that the worship carried on in the Temple had become corrupt and that they were the true wor-shipers of God. It was at the site of one of these communi-ties, at Qumran, that the valuable Dead Sea Scrolls were found in 1947.

Our discussion has now come to the period of history just before the birth of Christ. As we have seen, Jerusalem had already been the golden bowl of some empires. And there is more to come as we continue the amazing story.

The one hundred years of the Hasmonaean dynasty was one of the relatively brief periods of glory for the Jews in Jerusalem after the death of Solomon. During that time they ruled themselves and worshiped God in freedom. Unfortunately, that period also saw the rise of yet another world empire that would turn its evil attention toward Jerusalem.

Rome Dies at Jerusalem

In 63 B.C., a Roman army under Pompey the Great captured Jerusalem and made Judea part of the great, then-invincible Roman Empire. The city would remain essentially under Roman rule for more than six hundred years. Here was yet another of the world's dominant empires that was drawn to Jerusalem, would eventually destroy the city, and would therefore come under God's judgment.

Pompey's conquest of Jerusalem, however, did no great physical harm to the city. And under Rome's authority a new dynasty of kings with some local control was established. The first of these kings to be directly subject to Rome was Antipater. His son, who became king in 37 B.C., was Herod the Great, known to us today primarily as the king who tried to kill the baby Jesus because he thought the Christ-child to be a rival for his throne.

Herod the Great also did some good, however, for the city of Jerusalem. Not long after becoming king, he ordered and carried out a complete, magnificent, and lavish reconstruction of the Temple, a job requiring vast sums of money. The work was so extensive and complex that it was still not completed in the time of Jesus. Herod also built the Xystus, an open place surrounded by a gallery, a magnificent palace for himself, a hippodrome, a theater, and a large reservoir. Thus, despite his wickedness—which was truly extreme and extended far beyond his slaughter of Bethlehem's baby boys—Herod the Great actually did much of great value for the physical structure of Jerusalem.

During the first century A.D. religious conflicts led to bloody battles in Jerusalem and Judea. In addition, the Roman governors of Judea tended to be despotic and showed little respect for the Jewish religion. Their policies caused a violent insurrection against Rome starting in A.D. 66. It was led by the Zealots, a fanatical Jewish sect. Once again there was bloodshed in the land. (We read in the Bible that many people in Jesus' time, including many, if not all, of His disciples, thought and hoped *He* would lead such an armed revolt against Rome.)

Nero, the Roman emperor at that time, sent an army under his general Vespasian to stop the revolt. Before he finished the job, however, Vespasian returned to Rome to become emperor himself. He left the job of defeating the Zealots to his son, the general Titus, who also was to become an emperor of Rome.

Titus did his job very well, systematically crushing the revolt. In A.D. 70 he put Jerusalem under siege. He urged the city to surrender, even sending the Jewish historian Josephus to try to convince the city's leaders of the wisdom to surrender. But the city refused to surrender, so in August Titus finally entered the city in a terrible battle. He captured and devastated it, destroying the Temple, leveling its buildings, and throwing down its walls. The streets of the city literally ran with blood. Jerusalem was left in absolute ruin, once again a pile of rubble, and so it would remain for many years.

36

The final fortress of the Zealots, Masada, fell to the Roman legions in A.D. 73. The story of that place and time is a monument to man's yearning for freedom, and it provides a rallying point for the Jews to this day. Those who are not already familiar with the story should look it up in a history book; it is truly inspiring.

The Roman emperor Hadrian visited the city, still largely in ruins, in about A.D. 130 and began its reconstruction. From 132–35, however, the Jews once again rebelled violently against Roman rule. This time the insurrection was led by a man named Simon Bar-Cocheba. The Jews fought desperately and were successful for a time. Eventually, however, the revolt was put down, and Judea was once again at the mercy of Rome.

Hadrian was not merciful, and although he continued the rebuilding of Jerusalem after the rebellion, he changed the name of Judea to Syria Palaestina and the name of Jerusalem to Aelia Capitolina. Further, he made Jerusalem a pagan city and forbade Jews to enter it upon pain of death. Persecution of Jews became common throughout the empire.

The fall of Judea also widened the division between the Jews and the followers of the new Christian religion. Christianity grew increasingly influential in the succeeding years, and in 313 the Roman emperor Constantine I accepted Christianity for himself and made it the official religion of the empire. Constantine made Jerusalem a Christian city and built the Church of the Holy Sepulcher over the place believed to be the site of the tomb where Christ had been buried.

After a visit to the city by the Byzantine empress Eudocia, Jews were finally allowed back into Jerusalem in 438, following a forced absence of three hundred years. Eudocia

37

was also responsible for the building of the Church of Saint Stephen north of the city and the rebuilding of the city's ancient southern wall.

During the reign of Justinian I (527–65), a revolt in Samaria devastated the environs of Jerusalem; and a number of Christian churches were destroyed, yet another episode in the city's violent history. Justinian was the builder of the great Church of Saint Mary on the temple hill.

Just why God allowed Rome to continue in power to abuse Jerusalem for so many years is not clear. As we will see in chapter 5, there were certain aspects of the Roman occupation that facilitated the spread of the early Christian church throughout the world, and that may have partly accounted for God's patience. In any event, we know that the fate of Rome was sealed when it first determined to subjugate and abuse God's chosen city.

We might pause at this point to reflect on how many times Jerusalem had already been invaded and fought over by that time in its history, its walls broken through, its people starved under siege and then put to the sword, sold into slavery, or sent away from their homes and land into exile. Many times Jerusalem's buildings had been burned to the ground, its Temple leveled and looted. Americans, apart from our Civil War, have virtually no experience with such things in our brief two hundred years as a nation. While wars rage in much of the rest of the world, we live in freedom and peace, for which we should thank the Lord. But we cannot take our freedom for granted, as we will see in the last chapter.

Even though Jerusalem suffered many invasions and much violence and hardship, we should note that in each case, even when the city lay in ruins for years at a time, *God never let the city die*. He has always been faithful to preserve her, right up to the present, and He always will be. Babylon and Persepolis, two great capitals of world empires, among many others, are now nothing more than deserted piles of debris, but Jerusalem always rises from the rubble.

The Rise of Islam

In the early 600s, Muhammad founded the Islamic religion in Mecca, a city in what is now Saudi Arabia, and Muslims soon set out to conquer the world for Allah. In 637 an Arabic Muslim army under the caliph (successor to the prophet Muhammad) Omar I invaded Palestine and besieged and conquered Jerusalem. Arabs controlled the city for most of the next five hundred years.

From 687–91, the caliph Abd-al-Malik, one of a group of successive caliphs known as the Umayyads, built a most important building, the Dome of the Rock. This mosque is built on the peak of Mount Moriah, the temple mount, the site of the temples of Solomon, Zerubbabel, and Herod. Specifically, it is built over the rock believed to be the altar place of the Temple. As noted earlier, it is also the place believed to be, by tradition, the site of Abraham's offering up his son Isaac. Muslims believe Abraham went to that site to sacrifice his son Ishmael, the father of the Arabic peoples. Muslims also believe Adam and Eve offered sacrifices to God there.

Finally, and most important to the Muslims, they believe that Muhammad ascended into heaven on his winged horse, El Baruck ("lightning"), from the summit of the mount, the rock in the center of the Dome of the Rock. They say that when Muhammad ascended, the rock began to go up with him. An angel appeared, however, and held down the rock.

The fingerprints of the angel can still be seen on the side of the rock, Muslims claim, as well as the footprints of Muhammad. It is because of this belief about the ascension of the prophet from the rock that Muslims hold the Dome of the Rock, and Jerusalem generally, to be the third most holy place in the world, following only Mecca and Medina.

During the next millenium, control of Jerusalem passed from Egyptians to Syrians to Turks and back again, all of them Muslim. Most of that time, Jerusalem was largely neglected and allowed to decay.

Under the rule of the Seljuk Turks, however, beginning in 1071, Christians in Jerusalem were actively mistreated, and the Church of the Holy Sepulcher was destroyed. Those events led to the Crusades, which saw a Christian army, made up largely of French and Belgian troops, journey to Palestine to liberate Jerusalem from Muslim control.

The Crusaders succeeded in 1099, having laid siege to the city. Once they captured it, they put to death many of its Muslim and Jewish inhabitants. Other Jews and Muslims were taken prisoner and sold into slavery. Whatever their qualities, the Crusaders were not merciful, even to God's chosen people.

But Jerusalem was once again a Christian-controlled city. Streams of pilgrims came from Europe, and the population increased considerably. The Dome of the Rock was made into a Christian church. Jerusalem was made the capital of what was called the Latin Kingdom.

Crusader control did not last all that long, however. In 1187, Muslims retook the city from the Crusaders and removed all signs of the Crusader occupation. That led to subsequent Crusades, and Crusaders did capture the city and hold it briefly for one last time. Muslim forces drove them out for good in 1244.

To the Present

In 1517, Palestine was captured by Sultan Selim I of Turkey's Ottoman Empire. Except for a brief period, Turkey then held the land until the end of World War I. The most permanent accomplishment of the Turkish occupation was the rebuilding of Jerusalem's walls by Suleiman I ("the Magnificent"), son of Selim I, in approximately 1542. The remains of those walls are the walls still standing around the Old City of Jerusalem. The walls are two and a half miles long, average forty feet in height, and contain thirty-four towers.

Shortly after the outbreak of World War I, Turkey entered the war on the side opposite England and France; and the British and French consulates in Jerusalem were closed. England and her allies were victorious; and the British, with their French and Italian allies, entered Palestine under General Edmund Allenby. The British and allied troops seized and entered Jerusalem on December 9, 1917, ending almost seven hundred years of Muslim control.

Allenby's capture of Jerusalem was unusual and deserves special attention. Early on the morning of December 9, Allenby sent two reconnaissance planes over the city to scout the Turkish defenses. It was the first time in history that planes had flown over Jerusalem. Much to their surprise, the pilots discovered the Turks had deserted the city, leaving it wide open. The British were able to march in and take over the city without firing a single shot.

General Allenby had spent the previous day in prayer in anticipation of the expected battle for Jerusalem. His prayers, coupled with the amazing discovery by the scout planes, bring to mind the words of Isaiah 31:5: "Like birds flying about,/ So will the LORD of hosts defend Jerusalem./

Defending, He will also deliver it;/ Passing over, He will preserve it."

Sadly, the awesome British Empire of which Allenby was a part would also suffer a fatal blow while tampering with Jerusalem. The story of Britain's fall, which is especially intriguing because the events unfolded before the eyes of many of us who are still alive, will be discussed more fully in the last chapter.

3

Jerusalem and Jesus

A special facet of the history of Jerusalem for all Christians is the part the city played in the life and ministry of Jesus Christ, our Savior. He is the central focus, the essential part, of our faith; for apart from Him there is no Christianity. Therefore, it is only fitting that we concentrate for a short while on the relationship of Jerusalem to Jesus, who will one day establish an everlasting empire there.

We really need to begin this story even prior to Jesus' birth. For it was in Jerusalem that the birth of Jesus' forerunner, the one who would announce His coming and prepare the way for Him, was made known. I am referring to the birth of John the Baptist as it was prophesied by the angel Gabriel in Luke 1:8–20.

The story is familiar. John's parents, Zacharias and Elisabeth, were getting old, and they had no children because Elisabeth was barren. One day, however, as Zacharias, a priest, was serving in the Temple, Gabriel appeared to him and told him John would be born " ' "to turn the hearts of the fathers to the children," and the disobedient to the wisdom of the just, to make ready a people prepared for the Lord' " (Luke 1:17).

Zacharias doubted Gabriel, which from a human perspective is understandable, considering the ages of Zacharias and Elisabeth and her infertility.

And Zacharias said to the angel, "How shall I know this? For I am an old man, and my wife is well advanced in years." And the angel answered and said to him, "I am Gabriel, who stands in the presence of God, and was sent to speak to you and bring you these glad tidings. But behold, you will be mute and not able to speak until the day these things take place, because you did not believe my words which will be fulfilled in their own time" (Luke 1:18–20).

John the Baptist was born and fulfilled the role for which God created him. So, too, did Jesus Christ when He was born in Bethlehem, a small town only about six miles south of Jerusalem. He, God of God, the second Person of the Trinity, was born into the human race for many reasons, the most important of which was to die in Jerusalem thirty-three years later for our sins, taking upon His sinless self the righteous judgment of God that we deserve.

After Jesus was born, His parents took Him to the Temple to present Him to the Lord and purify Mary, as prescribed in the Mosaic Law.

According to that law, the new mother of a male child was considered unclean. On the boy's eighth day he was circumcised, but the mother remained unclean for another thirty-three days, after which she presented a burnt offering and a sin offering for her cleansing (see Lev. 12:4–6). The fact that Mary and Joseph brought two turtledoves for Mary's sacrifice shows they were poor, for that was the least-expensive acceptable sacrifice.

While the family was in the Temple, they encountered two remarkable people who confirmed that Jesus was to be the Savior. The first of these was Simeon. The Bible tells us only that he was "just and devout, waiting for the Consolation of Israel, and the Holy Spirit was upon him. And it had been revealed to him by the Holy Spirit that he would not see death before he had seen the Lord's Christ" (Luke 2:25-26). He had been led to the Temple by the Holy Spirit while Jesus and His parents were there, and when he saw Jesus, he took Him in his arms and blessed God and Jesus' family (see Luke 2:27-35).

The second person was Anna, a prophetess who lived in the Temple, fasting and praying continually. When she saw Jesus, she likewise thanked the Lord (see Luke 2:36-38). All this was amazing to Mary and Joseph, even though they knew of the miraculous nature of Jesus' conception. The Bible tells us, "And Joseph and His mother marveled at those things which were spoken of Him" (Luke 2:33).

When Mary and Joseph had done all the Mosaic Law required, they took Jesus and returned to their home in Nazareth, where Jesus grew up. Since they were devout Jews, they returned to Jerusalem every year for the celebration of Passover. When Jesus was twelve, He went with His parents for the festive occasion.

At the age of thirteen, a Jewish boy became a "son of the commandment" and a full member of the religious community, an adult. Prior to that time, He would not be allowed to participate completely in the worship ceremonies of the Temple. However, boys were often allowed to go to the Temple a year or two before the thirteenth birthday, and that was the case with Jesus.

So far as we know, there was nothing out of the ordinary about Jesus' celebration of the Passover with His parents. When the festivities were over, Mary and Joseph started back to Nazareth with their relatives and friends who had gone to Jerusalem with them. They did not have Jesus with them, but they assumed He was with some of the other people in their group. But at the end of the first day's journey they could not find Him anywhere. He had stayed in Jerusalem (see Luke 2:42–44).

Being the father of three sons, I know exactly how Mary and Joseph must have felt. To lose track of a boy in a crowded city so far from home is a terrifying experience for a parent. As I have prayed to the Lord for guidance in finding my sons in such situations, I am sure Mary and Joseph asked God to watch over Jesus and help them find Him.

They went back to Jerusalem to look for Him, and they had to search for three long days before they found Him in the Temple. Every parent knows exactly what they felt—a conflicting set of emotions. On one hand, because they loved Him, they were tremendously relieved to have found Him and glad to see Him again. Who knows what could have happened to Him? On the other hand, they were upset with Him for staying behind and not letting them know what He was doing. As a rule, children ought not to do such things to their parents. Because we know our Savior never sinned, however, it may be there was just some misunderstanding between Him and His parents.

> And His mother said to Him, "Son, why have You done this to us? Look, Your father and I have sought You anxiously." And He said to them, "Why is it that you sought Me? Did you not know that I must be about My Father's business?" (Luke 2:48–49).

Jesus had been listening to and asking questions of the "doctors," the scholars and teachers of the Jewish faith, and everyone who heard Him was amazed at the depth of understanding He displayed (see Luke 2:46–47). Here in Jerusalem was the first public demonstration of His spiritual wisdom recorded in the Bible. After that incident He returned to Nazareth with His parents and was subject to them while He grew into full manhood (see Luke 2:51–52).

Jesus' Public Ministry

The next recorded visit of Jesus to Jerusalem took place approximately nineteen years later, after He was a grown man and had already begun His public ministry, when He again went up to celebrate Passover. It may well be that He had visited Jerusalem for Passover in the intervening years, but the Bible is silent on the matter.

While in Jerusalem on this occasion, Jesus drove the money changers out of the Temple with a scourge for the first time, chasing away the animals that were for sale for sacrificial use and overturning the sellers' tables. The story is very familiar to us, but we must not let familiarity cause us to lose sight of the terrible thing that was going on.

The Temple was meant to be a place for the worship of God, and Antiochus Epiphanes desecrated it in one way, by sacrificing a ceremonially unclean animal on the altar. But here, with the approval of the priests, was desecration of another kind. The Temple was being used as a place of business, a place to make money off the Jewish pilgrims who came to the Temple from distant places and so had not been able to bring sacrificial animals with them. Jesus was understandably and rightly angry with them, and He took bold action to cleanse God's house. Note that the Jews' response was not thanks or repentance. Rather, they asked Him, in effect, "Who do You think You are? What authority do You have to do that?" (see John 2:13–18).

When we read this account in the Bible, we must keep in mind that our bodies are now the temple of the Holy Spirit (see 1 Cor. 6:19). And when He moves to cleanse our lives of those things we have allowed to take root that hinder our worship of Him, we should not respond like the Jews but should instead thank Him and yield to His will, knowing it is for His glory and our good.

While in Jerusalem, Jesus also performed some unspecified miracles, and many people believed in Him (see John 2:23). It was also during this visit that Jesus had His nighttime interview with Nicodemus, a Pharisee (see John 3:1–21). On that night He explained what it means to be born again and made the statement that has become probably the most famous verse in all the Bible: "For God so loved the world that He gave His only begotten Son, that whoever believes in Him should not perish but have everlasting life" (John 3:16).

Jesus then left Jerusalem to travel and minister in various parts of Israel, and He did not return to the city until the next Passover. During this visit He healed the lame man at the Bethesda pool, the pool to which an angel came occasionally to stir up the water. Whoever was then first into the water was healed from whatever physical problem he had. This lame man had no one to help him get into the pool, however, so he could never get in first. Jesus asked him, "Do you want to be made well?" (John 5:6). He then ordered the man to get up and walk, "and immediately the man was made well, took up his bed, and walked" (John 5:9).

What was the reaction of the Jewish leaders? Did they rejoice in the man's healing or marvel at the amazing demonstration of God's compassion? Hardly. Instead, they told the healed man, "It is the Sabbath; it is not lawful for you to carry your bed" (John 5:10). They looked right past the miracle to that small violation of their religious law, and concentrated on it. Unfortunately, we in the twentieth century still tend to do the same thing, so we should not be too quick to judge. May God teach us to focus on what He is doing rather than on our traditions.

During that same visit to Jerusalem, Jesus claimed publicly to be equal with God. For that reason, along with His doing works of healing on the Sabbath, the Jewish leaders sought to kill Him (see John 5:17–18). They were unable to do so, however, because it was not yet the time appointed for Him by the Father.

After leaving Jerusalem, Jesus would return three more times. But before we look at those events, let's consider a couple of things related to Jerusalem that took place away from the city. First, the Scriptures tell us that the Pharisees were strongly opposed to Jesus, because they were more concerned with their traditions than they were with seeing God's will done. Their headquarters was Jerusalem, and they were so upset by Jesus' popularity and disregard for their traditions that, on occasion, groups of them would travel out from Jerusalem to where Jesus was ministering so they could chide Him for His "failure" to observe the religious law.

One of the confrontations between Jesus and Pharisees from Jerusalem is recorded for us in Matthew 15:1–20 and Mark 7:1–23. On that occasion, the Pharisees' complaint was that Jesus' disciples did not wash their hands properly before eating. The Jews had an elaborate handwashing ritual before eating; it was part of their religious observance. When the Pharisees saw the disciples eating without having first washed, they asked Jesus, "Why do Your disciples not walk according to the tradition of the elders, but eat bread with unwashed hands?" (Mark 7:5).

Jesus replied:

"Well did Isaiah prophesy of you hypocrites, as it is written: 'This people honors Me with their lips,/ But their heart is far from Me/ And in vain they worship Me,/ Teaching as doctrines the commandments of men' " (Mark 7:6-7).

He then went on to point out that while they insisted upon proper observance of even the most minute parts of their traditions, they used those same traditions to disobey the clear teaching of God's Word, as when they allowed a man to escape his responsibility to provide for his parents by saying his profits were dedicated to the Temple ("corban"; see Mark 7:9-13). He added at the end of that condemnation, "And many such things you do" (Mark 7:13).

Our Savior knew the hearts of those Pharisees, and He saw that their hearts were far from God. Indeed, if they had been true followers of God and true scholars of His Word, they would have recognized Jesus as the Messiah. He pointed out on several occasions that Moses, the revered lawgiver of ancient Israel, had written of Him; and He added, "For if you believed Moses, you would believe Me.... But if you do not believe his writings, how will you believe My words?" (John 5:46-47). Jesus had picked the right word for them when He called them hypocrites.

The second thing we want to look at is that Jesus, being fully God as well as fully man, knew well before His crucifixion that He was to die for our sins in Jerusalem. Several different times He had told this to His disciples, as in Matthew 16:21. "From that time Jesus began to show to His disciples how He must go to Jerusalem, and suffer many things from the elders and chief priests and scribes, and be killed, and be raised again the third day."

His disciples didn't believe and didn't really understand until after His resurrection, but Jesus knew full well what lay ahead for Him in Jerusalem. He knew, and He was willing to go and suffer in our place to satisfy the justice of God and reconcile us to Him. Luke 9:51 tells us that when the time came for Jesus to turn His full attention to His final and most important mission, "He steadfastly set His face to go to Jerusalem." Nothing would deter Him from giving Himself in love.

Jesus' next visit to Jerusalem was for the Feast of Tabernacles, or Booths. During that time He was the central character in a number of incidents that are very familiar to Christians—for example, His forgiving of the woman caught in adultery (see John 8:1-11). He described Himself as the Light of the World, the Good Shepherd, and the Door (see John 8:12; 10:1-21).

One of the most interesting things about this visit to Jerusalem concerned the Pharisees and chief priests and their usual opposition to Him. On this occasion they sent officers to arrest Him, but the officers returned empty-handed. When those officers were asked why they had not brought Jesus, they replied, "No man ever spoke like this Man" (John 7:46).

That made the Pharisees and chief priests even more indignant. They responded, "But this crowd [believers in Jesus] that does not know the law is accursed" (John 7:49).

Then, who should come to Jesus' defense but Nicodemus, himself a Pharisee, the same one who had come to Jesus at night (see John 7:50-51). We do not know for certain if Nicodemus had already committed his life to the Lord Jesus at that point. But if he hadn't done so by then, it was almost certain he had by the time of Jesus' death, approximately six months later. For when Joseph of Arimathea took the dead body of Jesus to bury it, Nicodemus came with a mixture of burial spices and helped Joseph prepare and then entomb the body (see John 19:38–42).

Such a bold action on Nicodemus's part undoubtedly put his position as a Pharisee in danger, but his love for the Savior was greater than his fear of the condemnation of his peers. May God grant that our love for Jesus today would also be stronger than our concern over the ridicule of people who are antagonistic to Him.

The other incident we want to highlight in this visit of Jesus to Jerusalem was His very clear statement of His deity in John 8:12–59. Throughout this passage, as Jesus was jousting verbally with the Pharisees, both He and they made repeated references to Abraham. They were boasting of the fact that they were descendants of Abraham. Jesus told them that if Abraham were truly their (spiritual) forefather, they would believe Him rather than want to kill Him.

This conversation came to a climax in the last four verses of the passage. Jesus first said to the Pharisees, "Your father Abraham rejoiced to see My day, and he saw it and was glad" (John 8:56). In other words, He was indicating He had personally seen Abraham several millennia before.

The Pharisees, not believing in Jesus' eternal deity, then logically asked, "You are not yet fifty years old, and have You seen Abraham?" (John 8:57).

Jesus' answer is one of the simplest yet most profound statements in all of Scripture: "Most assuredly, I say to you, before Abraham was, I AM" (John 8:58). My heart thrills every time I read that verse. Jesus was saying, in effect, "Abraham lived several thousand years ago, as you well know. But long before he was born, even to eternity past, I, God in the flesh, existed."

The Pharisees, still not believing Him, nonetheless understood exactly what He was saying, as evidenced by the fact that they immediately picked up stones to throw at Him and stone Him to death for blasphemy. It was not yet His time to die, however, so He miraculously passed through their midst untouched (see John 8:59). Shortly thereafter, He left Jerusalem to minister in other parts of Israel.

When Jesus next went to Jerusalem, it was to be His last visit before the time when He would go there to die. The specific occasion for His going this time was the Feast of Dedication, which to this day is celebrated in December, near the winter solstice. The feast is also known as the Feast of Lights, or Hanukkah, and it was instituted in 164 B.C. by Judas Maccabaeus to commemorate the cleansing and reopening of the Temple after its desecration by Antiochus Epiphanes in 167 B.C.

While in Jerusalem at that time Jesus again declared His divinity, His oneness with God. The disbelieving Jewish leaders once again accused Him of blasphemy and took up stones to kill Him (see John 10:22–38). If Jesus had been a liar, as they thought, they would have been right to stone Him for blasphemy. But Jesus told the truth, and they should have known it. And because it still was not His appointed time to die, He once again escaped from them (see John 10:39).

The Last Visit

After teaching and healing outside Jerusalem for a while, Jesus set His face toward the city for the last time. On His way there, just before His final week, He stopped as He often had at the home of Mary, Martha, and Lazarus in Bethany. Bethany is less than two miles east of Jerusalem on the road to Jericho, on the eastern slope of the Mount of Olives. Because Bethany is so close to Jerusalem, it was Jesus' home in Judea, and it was His home for His last visit to the Holy City.

During that final week, Jesus had supper one night in Bethany at the home of a man identified only as Simon the leper. The Bible doesn't tell us anything else about him, but it may be that he was someone Jesus had healed. Regardless, Martha was helping to serve the meal; and while Jesus ate, Mary came to Him with a vial of a very expensive perfume called spikenard. She used the ointment to anoint His head and feet, filling the house with its smell, and then she wiped His feet with her hair (see Matt. 26:6-7; John 12:1-3).

Jesus' disciples, particularly Judas, were indignant at this because they considered it wasteful. "To what purpose is this waste?" they said. "For this fragrant oil might have been sold for much and given to the poor" (Matt. 26:8-9). Judas's concern was not for the poor, as John tells us in his gospel: "This he said, not that he cared for the poor, but because he was a thief, and had the money box; and he used to take what was put in it" (John 12:6). So the disciples had mixed motives in objecting to Mary's action, but they were certainly right about the perfume's great value. Mark's gospel tells us it was worth three hundred denarii, which was approximately a full year's wages for a rural worker (see Mark 14:5).

Jesus, however, did not share His disciples' reaction to Mary's anointing. "Why do you trouble the woman?" He asked. "For she has done a good work for Me. For you have the poor with you always, but Me you do not have always. For in pouring this fragrant oil on My body, she did it for My burial" (Matt. 26:10-12). In other words, it seems that Mary, unlike the twelve disciples, believed Jesus when He said He was soon going to die; and this was her way of expressing her love for the Savior and saying she believed. We should also note that Jesus' statement about the poor did not indicate callousness on His part. Rather, He was saying there would always be opportunity to help the poor, but shortly there would be no more chance to minister to Him as Mary had done.

It was right after that anointing that Judas went to the chief priests in Jerusalem and agreed to betray Jesus (see Matt. 26:14–16).

The rest of Jesus' last visit to Jerusalem is a familiar story that could easily fill a book by itself, and we cannot take the space here to discuss it in detail. We must not, however, let our familiarity with the events of the week—His triumphal entry, His teaching, His betrayal, His trial, His crucifixion, His resurrection—cause us to become indifferent to them, for they are the climax of His life and the means of our salvation. In God's precious eternal city, the holy God in human form bore our sins on the cross and then rose from the grave, victorious over death, three days later.

It is for this part of Jerusalem's long history that the city is the most wonderful place on earth to believers all over the world through all the generations of the church. And it is to this same city that the glorified Jesus will one day return!

4

Jerusalem and the Church

After the death of Jesus, the eleven apostles and His other followers suddenly found themselves without a leader. They were despondent and without hope. Then came the glorious news that He had been seen alive, but they refused to believe it. Sure enough, though, over the next forty days He revealed Himself in His resurrected body to many of them, speaking to them about the kingdom of God (see Acts 1:3).

Then He ascended into heaven, to intercede for us with the Father. Before He went, however, He commanded the apostles not to leave Jerusalem, but to wait for the Father's promise that He had given them (see Acts 1:4). He told them, "For John truly baptized with water, but you shall be baptized with the Holy Spirit not many days from now" (Acts 1:5). The disciples, about 120 of them (see Acts 1:15), stayed together in Jerusalem and waited. And while they waited, one of the things they did was to choose some-one to replace Judas among the twelve apostles. The man chosen was Matthias, one of Jesus' followers from the very beginning (see Acts 1:21–26).

Finally the great day arrived, the day of Pentecost, the official birthday, we might say, of the Church. The Holy Spirit came and took up permanent residence in human beings for the first time, and those so filled went out into the city speaking in languages (tongues) they did not know, as the

Spirit gave them power, to the amazement of Jews from every nation who were in Jerusalem and heard the gospel in their native tongues. It was such an exciting and important day that we want to look at it closely.

The story of Pentecost begins in Acts 2:1, and the first thing to notice there is that the day "had fully come." I love that phrase, because it tells me the birth of the Church was not an accident or a sidelight to history, but a planned, pre-arranged work of God.

In what sense had the day fully come? First, the Lord Jesus had lived, died, been resurrected, and ascended into heaven. All those things had to happen before the Holy Spirit could come (see John 16:7). And we know, too, that Jesus had come in "the fullness of the time" (Gal. 4:4)—that is, at just the right time chosen by God.

Second, the earth was physically ready for the growth of the Church, for the gospel to spread to every corner of the known world. The reason was the worldwide Roman Empire. As the Romans conquered every part of their world, they built and maintained roads to connect the various parts of the empire. Those roads made travel and commerce much easier than they had been before, and they also facilitated the movement of the mighty Roman legions. Because those legions were so strong and were able to maintain peace and safety in the empire, travel by Christian missionaries like Peter and Paul was much safer than it would have been a century before.

Third, the world of that day had a universal language, much as English is today, and that also contributed greatly to the effectiveness of traveling missionaries. Each land still had its native tongue, but there would be many in every country and in every large city who would be able to converse in the universal language, Greek. The Greek-speaking people could hear the gospel and pass it on to others; and they could also read the apostles' letters, written in Greek, to the local churches. Thus, the story of Jesus and doctrinal truths of the faith were spread rapidly to every corner of the world, regardless of the local languages.

In Acts 2:1, after it says the day "had fully come," it says "they were all...in one place." Who were those "all"? This phrase again speaks of the sovereignty of our God, because it suggests that everyone God wanted there was there. None whom He meant to be in that room was absent or even late. At the appointed time and place, they were all present and accounted for. None had slept late, and none had gone to the wrong address.

Just so, God is today calling all those He wants and needs in His service, and He is calling them to be in the place of His choosing. Those of us who are His children by spiritual rebirth must seek, find, and affirm the place He has picked for us. If we are not in that place, His work in this world will be hindered by our disobedience, and we will miss out on the fullness of the blessing He has in store for those who are in His perfect will.

Acts 2:1 also tells us "they were all *with one accord*" (emphasis added). This was important for the proper beginning of the Church, but it was a dramatic difference from the earlier experience of the disciples. Before, the mother of James and John, the sons of Zebedee, had come to Jesus and asked if her boys could have the places of greatest honor in His kingdom, making the other ten disciples angry. "And when the ten heard it, they were moved with indignation against the two brothers" (Matt. 20:24).

On other occasions, the proud and self-centered disciples had argued among themselves about which of them would be greatest in the kingdom (e.g., see Luke 9:46). They even argued about it during the Last Supper, just a few days before Jesus' death (see Luke 22:24). Far from being united in purpose, each disciple was seeking the best position for himself in Jesus' chain of command.

By the day of Pentecost, however, having witnessed the resurrected Lord Jesus, they had put their petty, selfish, divisive concerns behind them and were united in purpose. Again, the lesson for us is clear. Believers today must come together in purpose if our world is to be as fully blessed through the Church as God intends.

The Coming of the Holy Spirit

As Jesus' followers were gathered in one place, "suddenly there came a sound from heaven, as of a rushing mighty wind" (Acts 2:2). We do not know exactly what that sound was like, but perhaps those who have heard a tornado approaching, or the full strength of a hurricane, can better appreciate it. The sound must have been frightening and exhilarating at the same time. Maybe they thought the place was going to be blown down. On the other hand, they must have known, as the verse says, that the sound was from heaven, that God was about to do something, and that's always exciting.

The verse goes on to say, "and it [the sound] filled the whole house." The church of Jesus Christ began in a house, not a synagogue or any other official place of worship, and the lesson is that believers can worship anywhere. A magnificent cathedral might help to focus a person's attention on God, but such a building is no more holy or acceptable to God than the humblest home or apartment. What is important is the genuine desire to worship and glorify God.

Let us note finally in Acts 2:2 that the sound came and filled the house "where they were sitting." That suggests—and other passages of Scripture confirm—there is no one correct position for worship or prayer. One does not need to be face down on the floor, kneeling, standing, or even sitting, as the disciples were here. Some of the greatest spiritual experiences of my life have come while I was lying on my back in bed. We should not let anyone convince us we must adopt one particular pose. God is not against our being comfortable! The important consideration is where our minds and hearts are. If they are focused on Him, all is well.

Next, a tongue of fire appeared over the head of each disciple, and they were all filled with the Holy Spirit. They began to speak in tongues, as we noted earlier; and men of every nation heard the gospel, "the wonderful works of God" (Acts 2:11). Some people marveled at this amazing thing, but others mocked and accused the disciples of being drunk (see Acts 2:12-13).

Peter then stood up and explained that this speaking in tongues was a fulfillment of Old Testament prophecy and that Jesus was in fact the promised Messiah of God (see Acts 2:14-40). The Peter delivering this bold and powerful sermon was the same Peter who not many days before had denied his Lord three times because of fear and cowardice. Now he was filled with, and speaking in the power of, the Holy Spirit. As a result of this witness for Christ, about three thousand people were added to the church that day, truly one of the most memorable days in all of human history.

The bold preaching of Peter and others continued, accompanied by miraculous healings (see Acts 3; 5:12-16). The Spirit was working in a powerful way, and the church in Jerusalem soon grew to about five thousand men, plus women and children (see Acts 4:4).

Part of the witness to the world of that first church was the way they lived together. They ate, prayed, learned, and praised God together daily; and those who had possessions sold them to help meet the physical needs of other believers (see Acts 2:42–47; 4:32–37). All this was done gladly and willingly; no one was compelled to give. As a result of this sacrificial love and warm fellowship, the Church was "having favor with all the people. And the Lord added to the church daily those who were being saved" (Acts 2:47).

It was dangerous, however, to play games with the Holy Spirit in the matter of giving the proceeds of sale of one's possessions to the church, as illustrated by the well-known story of Ananias and Sapphira. They sold a piece of land and brought part of the proceeds to the apostles, but they lied and said what they were giving was everything they had received from the sale. As punishment for their dishonesty and, I am sure, as a warning to others, the Spirit struck them dead; and great fear understandably came on the whole church because of it (see Acts 5:1–11). We must realize here that they were not judged for holding back part of the proceeds of the sale; they were not obliged to give any of that money. Rather, as Peter pointed out, their sin was lying to the Holy Spirit.

Not surprisingly, the teaching of Jesus' resurrection and the growth of the church did not please the Jewish religious authorities, especially since they were the ones who had engineered His crucifixion. They brought in Peter and John and demanded to know what authority they had (see Acts 4). A little later, they had the apostles put in prison, from which an angel released them to preach again in the Temple (see Acts 5:17–20). So the authorities had them arrested again and said to them, "Did we not strictly command you not to teach in this [Jesus'] name? And look, you have filled Jerusalem with your doctrine" (Acts 5:28).

Then the apostles gave the reply that ever since has served as a model for Christians who have faced authorities trying to silence their witness for Christ or otherwise hinder their obedience to Him: "We ought to obey God rather than men" (Acts 5:29). Peter and the other apostles went on to accuse the Jewish leaders of Jesus' death and to proclaim Him to be the Savior.

At that point, the leaders would have had the apostles killed (see Acts 5:33), but an interesting irony of history came into play. The Pharisee whom God raised up to defend the apostles and secure their release with only a beating and a warning was Gamaliel, "a teacher of the law held in respect by all the people" (Acts 5:34). The ironic part of this is that Gamaliel, the respected teacher, had as one of his students the zealous young Pharisee Saul (see Acts 22:3).

Much of what Saul, later the apostle Paul, knew about God's Word he learned from this man Gamaliel who defended the apostles on this occasion. Part of his defense of them shows his wisdom, for he said of their teaching: "If this plan or this work is of men, it will come to nothing; but if it is of God, you cannot overthrow it—lest you even be found to fight against God" (Acts 5:38–39). He was right. The apostles' work was of God, and the Pharisees and the Sanhedrin could not overthrow it.

The Church Scatters

Opposition to the church did not end by any means, however, and before long the church grieved over its first martyr. Stephen was a man "full of faith and the Holy Spirit" (Acts 6:5), one of seven men in the church chosen to oversee the meeting of believers' physical needs so the apostles could concentrate on prayer and teaching (see Acts 6:1–7). He did great miracles and also preached, and some Jews who were antagonistic to the gospel arranged for other men to falsely accuse Stephen of blasphemy. Stephen was taken before the Sanhedrin, where in his defense, he gave a long and stirring sermon in which he recounted God's dealings with Abraham and his descendants. At the end, he also accused the council of murdering Jesus. Their guilty consciences were pricked by his words, but rather than repent they became murderously angry at him and "stopped their ears, and ran at him with one accord; and they cast him out of the city and stoned him" (Acts 7:57–58; see also 6:8–7:60).

The murder of Stephen was the beginning of serious trouble for the church. "At that time a great persecution arose against the church which was at Jerusalem; and they were all scattered throughout the regions of Judea and Samaria, except the apostles" (Acts 8:1).

As we go on in Acts 8, however, we see that even this uprising against the church was part of God's plan. We read in verse 4, "Those who were scattered went everywhere preaching the word." We can safely assume that some of the foreign Jews who heard the gospel in their native languages on the day of Pentecost took it back to their lands with them, but this scattering of the Jerusalem church was really the first missionary campaign, unplanned—from a human perspective—as it was. For these people had been trained under the apostles and so could teach others in Judea and Samaria the truths of the faith. Meanwhile, the apostles were still in Jerusalem to win and train others.

The apostles in Jerusalem, having walked with and been taught by Jesus Himself, also served as a council to oversee the growth of the church and resolve disputes. So Paul, after he was converted, went to Jerusalem to join the apostles. They were understandably suspicious of him at first, knowing the way he had persecuted the church. "As for Saul, he made havoc of the church, entering every house, and dragging off men and women, committing them to prison" (Acts 8:3). But later Paul won their confidence with the help of Barnabas, and he joined them (see Acts 9:26–29).

Likewise, after Peter had taken the gospel to the Gentiles and baptized some of them (the family of a Roman officer, no less) in obedience to God's command, he had to explain his actions to the church at Jerusalem and help them see that the gospel was, indeed, for Gentiles as well as Jews (see Acts 11:1–18).

One last example of this role of the apostles and the elders of the Jerusalem church comes in the dispute that arose over whether Gentiles who became Christians had to be circumcised like Jews. Certain Jewish Christians said circumcision was necessary, but Paul and Barnabas disagreed. Paul would write later to the church in Rome, "For he is not a Jew who is one outwardly, nor is that circumcision which is outward in the flesh; but he is a Jew who is one inwardly, and circumcision is that of the heart, in the Spirit" (Rom. 2:28–29).

The dispute was taken to the apostles and elders in Jerusalem, where both sides were argued strenuously. Then the apostles and elders made their decision based on their understanding of God's will, and the answer was that circumcision was not necessary. They drafted letters to that effect to be distributed to the scattered churches (see Acts 15:1–29). So the issue was resolved.

JERUSALEM: WHERE EMPIRES DIE

Even as Jerusalem remained the home of the mother Christian church, it also was still the home of the Jewish faith, and nonbelieving Jews continued to be hostile to the gospel, just as many of them are yet today. Thus, it is not surprising that James, the brother of John, one of the apostles, was murdered in Jerusalem, or that Peter was arrested there again and would have been killed if an angel had not miraculously released him (see Acts 12:1–18). So also was Paul later arrested and tried in Jerusalem, and from there he began his last journey, in chains, to Rome (see Acts 21:15–23:22).

Those were exciting times in Jerusalem when the church was born, when the Holy Spirit came upon men and empowered them to speak in tongues, heal the sick, preach the gospel with great boldness, and begin to spread the good news through all the earth. We may wish we could have been there to see it all and participate in the thrill of those days. But the sovereign God has called us to live and serve Him in this age, and it, too, is an exciting time. For the Holy Spirit is still at work in and through believers who are willing to be used to spread the gospel of Jesus Christ to every part of the world.

May the Lord grant that we sense the challenge of this moment and step forth boldly in the power of the Spirit to win this age for His kingdom.

5

The Wanderers Return

On Friday, May 14, 1948, David Ben-Gurion, leader of the unofficial Jewish government in Palestine, stood before a microphone in a Tel Aviv museum and formally declared the existence of the new state of Israel. It was a moment of high drama, the climax of almost two thousand years of Jewish hopes to once again live in their own sovereign nation in the land of Abraham, Joshua, and David. It was also one of the most significant fulfillments of biblical prophecy in this or any age. At the same time, it was only the beginning of the new Israel's desperate struggle to survive, for immediately the surrounding Arab nations invaded Israel in an attempt to drive the overwhelmingly outnumbered Jews into the Mediterranean Sea.

The Arab efforts were doomed, however, because God was at work on the side of Israel. Just how the new nation came into being, and how it not only survived but thrived despite tremendous obstacles, are the subjects to be explored in this chapter. We will also see how Israel regained complete control of Jerusalem. It is truly one of the most exciting chapters in the annals of history.

Before World War II

We saw in chapter 3 that the Jews had not enjoyed any

kind of self-rule in their homeland since the conquest of Jerusalem by the Roman general Titus in A.D. 70. For the last four hundred years prior to the British general Allenby's capture of Jerusalem in 1917, the city and all of Palestine had been under the control of the Turkish Ottoman Empire. The Turks were in command when the story of the new Israel began.

Over the course of the centuries, Jews had made their way back to Palestine in small numbers from various parts of the world. Zionism, the worldwide movement for an independent Jewish state in Palestine, began to take hold in the nineteenth century with the start of an organized Jewish settlement. The first modern Jewish agricultural colony, Petah Tiqwa, was founded about 1870, and others were established soon after that.

Zionism became a well-organized movement in the last decade of the nineteenth century under the guidance of Theodor Herzl, an Austrian writer. He made it an effective political force in numerous countries, including the United States. The cause was helped in the first decade of the twentieth century, ironically, by pogroms (organized massacres of Jews) and other acts of anti-Semitism in Czarist Russia and various parts of Eastern Europe. Such actions led many Russian Jews to emigrate to Palestine, and they caused Jews in other nations to see in Zionism the only real solution to anti-Semitism.

Meanwhile, the early Jewish settlements in Palestine were being attacked occasionally by Arabs, so a loosely organized defensive group known as *Hashomer* (Hebrew for "Watchmen") was formed. This group became the forerunner of the Israeli army. Arab opposition to the establishment of a new Israel would prove to be one of the great obstacles to the creation of the nation.

The other primary obstacle was Great Britain, which took control in 1917. In that same year, Arthur James Balfour, British foreign secretary at the time, said that Britain pledged to support the establishment of a Jewish "national home" in Palestine.

That pledge was incorporated in the mandate the League of Nations gave Britain in 1922 to occupy, govern, and "protect" Palestine. England was to "facilitate" Jewish immigration and settlement there. However, the mandatory government (the British administrative government for Palestine) divided the area into two parts, with the area east of the Jordan River designated a separate legal entity called Transjordan. Jews were forbidden to settle in or even enter Transjordan.

When the Nazis came to power in Germany in 1933, Jews began to experience new persecution in Europe, and increasing numbers of them left for Palestine. Arabs in Palestine had already begun to organize political opposition to Zionism, but with the rise in Jewish immigration, they resorted to rioting in 1936. For the next three years, there were killings almost every day.

In response, Palestinian Jews organized two clandestine armed forces (the British made all armed forces but their own illegal). The *Haganah* (Defense), an underground army, replaced the Hashomer in 1936. It was dedicated solely to defending Jewish people and property. In 1937, however, a second and smaller group, the *Irgun Zvai Leumi* (National Military Organization), was formed, and it was far more aggressive. It carried out offensive retaliatory attacks against Arabs, believing the Arab riots were encouraged by the British and would not be stopped by self-defense alone. One reason for British sympathy toward the Arabs was that Britain did not want to upset the Arabs surrounding the Suez, where it had control of some oil fields. (Throughout modern Israel's brief life, the support of her allies, including the United States, has been tempered by those allies' desire not to alienate the oil-rich Arabs.)

In 1939, claiming it needed to find a way to restore peace in Palestine, England issued a policy statement saying a Jewish national home had already been established there, since there was a large and flourishing Jewish community. That implied that the promise it had made of a Jewish "national home" did not mean a sovereign state but only a functioning community. And, by that definition, Britain claimed it had already fulfilled that part of its mandate.

Then, saying Britain had to respect the wishes of the "local inhabitants," the policy statement restricted further Jewish immigration to seventy-five thousand over the next five years, thus making certain Arabs would remain in the majority in Palestine. The statement also strictly limited Jewish purchases of Palestinian land.

Understandably, Arabs were pleased with the policy statement, and Arab violence came to an almost complete stop. The Jews, on the other hand, were understandably disturbed, and the Irgun changed the target of its attacks from the Arabs to the British.

From World War II to Independence

When World War II broke out, the Jewish armed forces found themselves, ironically, allied with the British against the Axis powers. Both the Haganah and the Irgun joined Britain in the war effort, and about thirty thousand Palestinian Jews joined the British Middle Eastern forces.

The Irgun was split in 1940 when a group that became

known as the "Stern Group" went off on its own. Though its leader, Abraham Stern, believed that the immigration of Jews from Europe was of greatest importance, the British forces during the war all but stopped entirely such immigration. To try to force the British to change their policies, the Stern Group launched a campaign of assassinations against British officials.

After the war, when the extent of the Holocaust became known, Zionism experienced a new drive, and Palestinian Jews urged that the concentration camp survivors be allowed in. Britain refused, however, and the would-be immigrants were forced to jam into ships and try to run the English naval blockade of Palestine. When the British warships spotted such an illegal ship, they would follow it to port. Then, when the relieved and tearful immigrants finally touched their feet to the soil of Palestine, British soldiers would arrest them, jam them back into transports, and ship them to detainment camps on the island of Cyprus.

Sometimes the captured immigrants weren't even fortunate enough to be sent to Cyprus. In the most publicized case, the British sent passengers from the immigration ship *Exodus* back to Germany.

The immigrants defying the British restrictions and blockade believed, correctly, that they had a higher mandate than England's. In the "passports" issued them by Jewish authorities was this passage from Ezekiel 37:25: "Then they shall dwell in the land that I have given to Jacob My servant, where your fathers dwelt; and they shall dwell there, they, their children, and their children's children, forever."

With that sense of destiny, the Jewish immigrants continued to try to run the British blockade, and they stole through by the dozens and the hundreds. God was at work to bring His people back to their land, and no power on earth—the British nor the Arabs—could stop them. As the immigrants got in, they multiplied and worked hard to make the dusty land productive.

As the illegal immigrants poured into Palestine, the British became more harsh, and the Arabs grew more concerned. The Jews were already resentful over Britain's refusal to relax its immigration restrictions, and that plus this new English harshness led to more anti-British fighting. Both the Stern Group and the larger and stronger Irgun asserted that because the British administration had violated the immigration and land settlement provisions of its mandate, it had become an unlawful occupying power.

Thus, beginning in 1945, steadily mounting violence became the order of the day. The Jews fought both the Arabs and the British. Palestine became the last place on earth where British soldiers were dying, and it was for a cause that the world generally and even most Britons did not support. The Jewish Agency, the official Zionist and unofficial governmental organization of the Jews in Palestine, denounced what it called the terrorism of the Irgun and the Stern Group; but it was also helped by their activities. David Ben-Gurion, the leader of the Jewish Agency, told the British he could not prevent Jewish violence unless concessions were made.

As these things were going on in Palestine, Jews and their supporters in America were giving more money for the support of the Zionist cause and pressuring the United States government to urge a change in English policy.

Tensions came to a head in early 1947 with the imminent execution of a captured Irgun leader. In March, the British army imposed martial law on Tel Aviv and the Jewish sections of Jerusalem. When four captured Irgunists were hanged, the Irgun retaliated by hanging two British soldiers.

That incident produced an uproar in England and a call for a change in Palestinian policy. But the mandatory government found itself in a quandary. It feared that more repressive measures against the Jews would only bring about an alliance between the moderate and militant groups. On the other hand, it did not want to allow greater Jewish immigration for fear of upsetting the Arabs. So the British government passed the ball in April 1947 by asking the United Nations to solve the problem.

A special meeting of the United Nations General Assembly resulted in the assigning of an eleven-nation commission to study the problem. On August 31 the commission issued a report recommending the termination of the British mandate and the partitioning of Palestine into separate Arab and Jewish states, with an international zone between that would include Jerusalem and the immediate surrounding area. On November 29 the General Assembly voted to implement such a plan and create the two new states. The British said they would make their final, complete withdrawal from Palestine on May 15, 1948.

The creation of a Jewish state was totally unacceptable to the surrounding Arab nations. Everyone knew that as soon as the British were gone, the Arabs would attack Israel in an effort to destroy it. On the morning of November 30, 1947, the day after the United Nations vote, the secretary-general of the Arab League said, "This will be a war of extermination and a momentous massacre." The representative of the Palestinian Arabs added that the border between the two new states would be settled by "fire and blood."

Fighting started again in Palestine immediately after the United Nations vote. Groups of Arabs would attack Jewish farms and settlements, and the Jews would retaliate. The men of the Jewish military organizations met secretly to plan their defense. Getting arms was not easy; the Jews still represented no formal government at that point, plus the British had placed an embargo on the importation of weapons into Palestine. To get around that latter problem, those selling the arms broke down many of the weapons into their component parts and shipped them to Palestine in bits and pieces under official import permits for such allowable items as textile machinery.

By the spring of 1948, Jewish troops had driven Arab forces out of the coastal territory and seized a number of towns in Galilee, the northern part of Palestine west of the Jordan.

They were also preparing to take over all of Jerusalem. They had tapped into the British and Arab phone lines, so they knew when they should move into each important defensive position as the British pulled out on May 14. They had planned carefully, even making sure there was a two-gallon daily supply of water large enough to last 115 days for every Jew in Jerusalem.

The survival of the Jews in Palestine was still far from certain, however. They were badly outmanned and outgunned by the Arabs, and they estimated their chances of succeeding alone to be only fifty-fifty. The hope was that the United States might send troops to help defend them. The fear was that if the National Council, the unofficial government, declared statehood before the Arabs attacked in force, America would be less willing to send help.

With those concerns in mind, David Ben-Gurion called a last secret meeting of the Council to decide whether to proclaim statehood immediately. By a majority of just one vote, the Council decided to proceed, setting the ceremony for 4:00 P.M. on Friday, May 14. That way, the new nation would be in formal existence when the last British official left, and the new government also would not have to do political business on Saturday, the Jewish Sabbath.

Invitations to the declaration ceremony went to two hundred guests and members of the press, who were urged to keep the time and location secret so both the British troops and Arab snipers would stay away.

As the appointed time approached, the mood in the jammed hall was festive but subdued. Almost two thousand years of Jewish hopes were about to be fulfilled, but everyone knew a difficult fight and many lost lives lay ahead.

As Ben-Gurion walked into the auditorium, the emotional audience rose to sing the "Hatikvah," a song that would become the national anthem of the new Israel. The crowd was made up of all types of Israelis, including the descendants of those pious Jews who had never left the Holy Land, legal immigrants, illegal immigrants, and Sabras, children who had been born in Palestine to immigrant parents.

Ben-Gurion stood to speak under a portrait of Theodor Herzl. He held in his hands a synthetic parchment with his typed manuscript glued to it—there had been no time to get genuine parchment and have it properly inscribed. He began his speech, which was a defense of Israel's right to exist, with an appeal to history:

Eretz-Israel was the birthplace of the Jewish people. Here their spiritual, religious, and political identity was shaped. Here they first attained to statehood, created cultural values of national and universal significance and gave to the world the eternal Book of Books.

After being forcibly exiled from their land, the people kept faith with it throughout their Dispersion and never ceased to pray and hope for their return to it and for the restoration in it of their political freedom.

Thirty-two minutes later, Ben-Gurion concluded, "The right of the Jewish people to establish their state is irrevocable." The speech done, Ben-Gurion left the dais, feeling no joy. Instead, he was aware of the massed Arab armies already moving toward them. Later he would say, "I was thinking of only one thing: the war we were going to have to fight."

Indeed, just the day before, 148 Jews had died at the kibbutz of Kfar Etzion when it was overrun by Arabs after months of siege. The settlers could have retreated in the face of imminent defeat, but they had not. They had stood their ground while the surrounding hills were covered with advancing Arabs. Ben-Gurion had ordered them to stand—all the kibbutzim would stand. The Arabs would have to fight for every inch they took, and they would advance only over the bodies of *dead Jews* who loved freedom more than life.

The Fight to Survive

Almost simultaneously with the formal announcement of the new Israel, the regular armies of the surrounding Arab states crossed the frontier between nations and attacked Jewish settlements. Lebanon, Syria, Iraq, and Transjordan came from the north and east, and Egypt from the south. Transjordan threw its best troops into the fight for Jerusalem, which was waged fiercely house-to-house. The Irgun and the Stern Group had kept many of their men in Jerusalem to fight for its control, but they were overwhelmed and forced to surrender fourteen days later. The population of the ancient Jewish quarter of the Old City had to leave and did not return for nineteen years.

The state of Israel began its official existence at midnight on May 15. Eleven minutes later, United States President Harry Truman extended formal diplomatic recognition. But there would be no American troops.

The initial fighting went badly for the Israelis. Their supply of arms was inadequate, and they suffered heavy casualties. A United Nations-arranged cease-fire in June and early July allowed them to regain strength, however, and when it ended they went on the attack, where they remained until the hostile Arab states conceded defeat and signed armistice agreements in the spring of 1949. The agreement with Jordan (its name was changed in 1949) left control of New Jerusalem in Israeli hands and the Old City in Jordanian hands. The fighting had driven nearly one million Arabs, who are now the Palestinian refugees, from their homes.

In December 1949 the U.N. General Assembly repeated its 1947 decision to put all of Jerusalem under international control. Both Jordan and Israel, which joined the United Nations in May 1949, opposed the decision; and Israel said it intended to keep New Jerusalem in defiance of the United Nations. On January 23, 1950, Jerusalem became the capital of Israel.

Within minutes of declaring its independence in May 1948, Israel had passed its first law, which opened the way for Jews to immigrate. Immediately a flood of immigrants, previously kept out by the British, poured into Israel. During the first four months, 50,000 European Jews arrived, and many more followed. By the end of 1951, the new state had taken in 687,000 people, more than doubling the population.

The vast ingathering strained the nation's resources almost to the breaking point. At first, new arrivals were kept in deserted Arab villages or tent cities. Within a year, however, the care of the immigrants had become a well-organized operation; and new immigrants were being actively recruited, brought to Israel, and established there. Much of the money used for these efforts was raised in the United States.

In the first three years of statehood, the Israeli government built 78,000 new dwellings and started 345 new villages and farm communities, doubling the number of the country's settlements. For all that effort, however, the newcomers still had to work hard to make a living, adjust to the hot climate and arid land, and learn Hebrew, the national language. But they had come home to the land of their forefathers, and they were willing to work.

There is much that could be said about the history of the new Israel from 1951 to the present, but that is not our purpose here, and we will confine our discussion to a brief look at how Israel took control of the Old City of Jerusalem in 1967.

The conquest of Jerusalem was part of the lightning-quick, astounding Six-Day War of June 1967. Determined to destroy the Israelis, Egypt, Iraq, Syria, and Jordan amassed tanks, troops, and planes in the Sinai desert next to the Israeli border. President Nasser of Egypt demanded that the U.N. Emergency Force leave the area at once. Without consulting the Security Council or anyone else, U.N. Secretary-general U Thant immediately withdrew the forces. The Arab leaders bombarded their people with rhetoric and worked them into a frenzy of war hysteria.

"The West seemed to be either paralyzed or indifferent, while the Russians were backing the Arabs to the hilt,"[1] Golda Meir wrote in her autobiography. The Western world wrung its hands and did nothing.

Meanwhile, the people of Israel made grim preparations. The women and children turned their basements into air-raid shelters. Parks in every city were consecrated for possible use as mass cemeteries.

Golda Meir recalled: "Not one Jew left Israel during those awful weeks of waiting. Not one of the mothers in the settlements below the Golan Heights or in the Negev took her children and ran. . . . Hundreds upon hundreds of Israelis who had gone abroad returned, although no one had called them back."[2]

On the morning of June 5, a series of perfectly planned and executed Israeli air strikes on key airfields in Egypt, Syria, and Jordan virtually wiped out the Arab air forces, leaving the Arab ground forces, stationed in open desert, exposed and vulnerable to air attack. In those six short days, the Israelis took all the Sinai peninsula from Egypt, the west bank of the Jordan river, including the Old City of Jerusalem from Jordan, and the Golan Heights in the north from Syria.

For the first time since the nation's founding in 1948, Jews were able to worship at the Wailing Wall and move back into the Old City. It was a stunning victory, and it established Israel as the major power in the Middle East. (Since then, Israel has given most of the Sinai back to Egypt, but it still holds the other two large parcels of land.) It also made Jerusalem a unified city under Jewish control for the first time in more than two thousand years.

---

[1] Golda Meir, *My Life* (New York: G. P. Putnam's Sons, 1975), 357.
[2] Ibid., 360.

JERUSALEM: WHERE EMPIRES DIE

There are many biblical prophecies that predicted God would again draw His people Israel to His Holy Land in the last days, and the creation of the new Israel thirty-five years ago in fulfillment of those promises is one of the most convincing arguments that we are, indeed, in the end times. We have already seen the prophecy from Ezekiel 37 that was quoted in unofficial Israeli passports prior to 1948; and Ezekiel 33–48, which speaks of the restoration of Israel, is one of the most exciting prophetic passages in the Bible.

The lesson for us here is that everything in the history of peoples and nations is working out according to God's plan. Nothing surprises Him, and nothing and no one can thwart His intentions. When His appointed time came for the restoration of Israel in Palestine, the success of Zionism was inevitable. And as we shall focus on in later chapters, He has chosen to reveal much of what He has ordained for Israel and Jerusalem in the future to us in the Bible. Already, by His power, the city of God has been restored to Israel. The state is set for that time when, in God's perfect scheme, the last two world empires will march against Jerusalem.

6

The Exalted City

The nicknames given to cities tell us what images
come to people's minds when they think of those places.
For example, New York is known as "the Big Apple,"
which signifies that in many ways it is the most important
city in America and even the world. San Francisco is "the
City by the Bay"—beautiful San Francisco Bay with its famous seafood restaurants and magnificent Golden Gate
Bridge. Detroit is "Motor City" because it is home to the
nation's largest automobile makers.

In the same way, names given to Jerusalem indicate what
people and God think about the city. Many descriptive
names for Jerusalem are in previous chapters. It has been
called "the city of God" (Ps. 46:4), "the perfection of
beauty" (Ps. 50:2), and "the joy of the whole earth" (Ps.
48:2). These names clearly show Jerusalem to be a special,
even unique, city. In this chapter we will look at a few more
of the historical and biblical names for Jerusalem and see
what they tell us about this city where empires die.

Jerusalem has been called by different names by different
peoples down through history. The first reference to the city
that has been found is in a nineteenth-century B.C. text.
There the city is called *Ruschalimum*. An Egyptian name
from roughly the same period is *Urushamem*.

As time went on, the names used for the city began to re-
semble more closely the modern name. In fourteenth-cen-

tury B.C. hieroglyphs, for example, Egyptian pharaohs called it *Urusalim*, which means "foundation of Salem." Salem, which has also come to mean "peace" (from the Hebrew word for peace, *shalom*), was at that time a reference to the Canaanite god of dusk.

The early references of Jewish rabbis to the city call it *Yerushalayim*, a name also used in the Bible. This particular name has survived to the present, and it is still the official Hebrew name of the city.

Greek-speaking Jews were the first to call the city Jerusalem. Another name of Greek origin is *Hierosolyma*, which comes from the root word *hieros*, meaning "holy." Both these names are used in the New Testament.

By the time of Jesus, the understanding of *Jerusalem* as the "city of peace" was commonly accepted (e.g., see Luke 19:41–42). It is today easily the most popular interpretation of the name, because it reflects the hopes for the city of people everywhere who love her.

Looking at other biblical names for the city, we see first and unsurprisingly that Jerusalem was and is the chief and most important city in Israel. Chapter 2 showed that Jerusalem became the capital city under King David. We also see its significance, however, in a passage like 2 Chronicles 25:28, where it is simply identified as "the City of Judah."

In the period of history being covered in that part of the Scriptures, the nation of Israel had already been divided into two kingdoms, Israel and Judah, following the death of Solomon; and Jerusalem had remained the capital of Judah. And in the immediately preceding verse, Judah's King Amaziah had just been killed. Now, he was buried in "the City of Judah." Nothing more needed to be said—everyone would know that phrase referred to Jerusalem. No other city could possibly claim to deserve that title more than Jerusalem—it was *the* City of Judah.

Likewise, in Isaiah 33:20, Jerusalem is called "the city of our appointed feasts." Again, to what other city could such a designation possbily refer? Jerusalem was the center of Jewish worship, the home of the Temple and the priesthood. So such a phrase was all anyone needed to make clear reference to Jerusalem, the spiritual as well as political capital of Israel.

The city is also known in the Bible, and is still known today, as "the Holy City" (Neh. 11:1,18; Matt. 4:5). It is called that for several reasons. First, God has set His affection on Jerusalem in a special way. Second, it is the capital of His chosen people, the Jews. Third, and most important, it was and will be again the dwelling place of God on earth. For all these reasons, Jerusalem truly is the Holy City.

An interesting name given to Jerusalem in only one short biblical passage is "Ariel," which means "lion of God" (Is. 29:1-2,7). A lion is strong and courageous, an animal feared by all. It is appropriate that in that passage Jerusalem is also called "the city where David dwelt" (v.1), because David was Israel's greatest king and also a great warrior. Thus, his reign in Jerusalem was the time when "lion of God" would have been most fitting as a description for the city.

As we look at these names that have been used to exalt Jerusalem in the Bible, we should keep in mind that they reflect the love of God and His people much more than they reflect any deserved praise. The citizens of Jerusalem down through the centuries have rebelled against God and chosen the worship of idols over the worship of Him far more often than not.

Jesus one time sent His disciples out to preach repentance; and He told them that if any city would not receive their message, "It will be more tolerable for the land of Sodom and Gomorrah in the day of judgment than for that city" (Matt. 10:15). Sodom and Gomorrah were the wicked, sexually depraved cities that God destroyed with fire and brimstone in the time of Abraham (see Gen. 19). Yet here Jesus said those cities would fare better in the day of final judgment than a city that rejected His gospel.

By that standard, Jerusalem's inhabitants over the years have had much more reason to expect God's condemnation than they have had to expect His praise. The abundance of His praise and love, therefore, is a stirring testament to the depth of His mercy and grace and patience.

The example of God's grace and patience toward Jerusalem should be a great comfort to us, for even we who call on the name of the Lord Jesus often rebel against Him and give our love and devotion to things and people other than Him. How many times we turn our backs, only to find His arms of love are still wrapped around us! His love for us reflects the richness of His love, not our merits. His mercy and patience toward sinners truly are deserving of praise, and His name merits exaltation above all others.

Future Glory

Even as we consider the frequent rejection of God the Father and Son by Jerusalem, we should also look ahead to that time when Jesus will return and Jerusalem will finally become everything God wants her to be. Those events are predicted in the Bible, and we are also given names by which the city will then be known. The difference between the past and the future in terms of those names is that when

Christ reigns in Jerusalem, it will fully deserve its exalted names.

One of the names to be applied to Jerusalem in that future glory is "the city of righteousness" (Is. 1:26). Only through God's eyes of mercy would Jerusalem have been deserving of that title in the past, but it will one day be literally accurate. Likewise, the city will be known as "the faithful city" (Is. 1:21,26), and it will finally be just that. It will also become the "City of Truth" (Zech. 8:3), the "New Jerusalem" (Rev. 21:2), and "The Throne of the LORD" (Jer. 3:17).

A beautiful name for the glorious Jerusalem will be "The LORD Our Righteousness" (Jer. 33:16). It is such an appropriate name, because the emphasis is not on the city at all, but rather on God, whose glory will fill and illuminate it. To go to Jerusalem in that time will indeed be to go to God Himself.

Similarly, Jerusalem will be given the most wonderful name any city could be given: "The LORD Is There" (Ezek. 48:35). What could be better or more exciting for a city than to have God in it? How could a city be more appealingly known than as the place where God is?

The lesson for us is that if we have believed in Jesus Christ as our Lord and Savior, He is already resident within us in the Person of the Holy Spirit. The crucial question is then whether others recognize that fact by the way we live. Do they see His love and mercy when they look in our eyes? Do they see His compassion and devotion to the Father when they examine our lives? There is a popular Christian song in which the singer expresses the hope that when others look at her, they will say, "She's got her Father's eyes." That should be the fervent prayer of us all.

The deservedly exalted names of the future Jerusalem

also tell us that as imperfect as the city has been in the past, as unfaithful as her people have been to God, and as often as she has succumbed to evil, both self-inflicted and imposed by conquerors, God is still not done with her. In spite of all that, He has glorious plans for her that He will execute according to His perfect, sovereign timetable. He can and will make her the most magnificent city ever seen, despite her often inglorious past.

Likewise, even though we have been far from perfect, even though we have often proved unfaithful to our loving God, and even though we may be covered with scars both self-inflicted and caused by others, God has wonderful plans for us who are His children by adoption, plans that He will work out in His perfect time. And one day, our Father will bring us to glory, all through His marvelous grace. In that day, "God will wipe every tear from [our] eyes; and there shall be no more death, nor sorrow, nor crying; and there shall be no more pain" (Rev. 21:4).

7

The City Gates

For most of its history, Jerusalem has been a walled city, a fortress built over several hills, as was common for important ancient cities. Thus, whenever the city was put under siege, the people of Jerusalem locked themselves inside the city, and the attackers had to try to find a way in. The other option for attacking armies was to surround the city so no one and nothing could get in or out, then wait for the people inside to run out of food.

Although no city walls were impregnable, they did offer a formidable defense that was not easily or quickly overcome. As we saw in chapter 3, the present walls around the Old City, built in approximately 1542 by Suleiman I, average forty feet in height and contain thirty-four towers.

A city's walls naturally had gates to allow people and animals to move in and out. The gates served other functions as well in the ancient Middle East; at night they would be closed and guarded to protect the inhabitants. The gates usually consisted of double doors that were plated with metal. The plating was important, because plain wooden doors could be set on fire easily by an attacker.

One of the functions of city gates, including those of Jerusalem, was to serve as a place of business. There were often shops just inside a city's gates, and on market days the commerce would spill outside. Further, certain kinds of markets would be held outside specified gates on regular days, and a city's gates often became known for the markets usually held near them. In Nehemiah's day, for example, Jerusalem had gates known as the "Sheep Gate," the "Fish Gate," and the "Horse Gate" (Neh. 3:1,3,28).

The city gates were also a place for the elders to conduct legal business. In God's giving of the Law to Israel through Moses in Deuteronomy 16:18, God said, "You shall appoint judges and officers in all your gates, which the LORD your God gives you, according to your tribes, and they shall judge the people with just judgment." So when Boaz went to redeem Ruth from her closer kinsman, for example, he discussed the matter with his kinsman and the elders at the city gate (see Ruth 4:1–12).

Finally, a city's gates were a place where people went to hear news, gossip, important announcements, and, in the case of Israel, to hear the reading of the Law on at least one occasion (see Neh. 8:1–3). In the time of Judah's king Hezekiah, when Hezekiah learned that the Assyrian king Sennacherib was going to attack Jerusalem, Hezekiah "set military captains over the people, gathered them together to him in the open square of the city gate" (2 Chr. 32:6). There at the gate, he encouraged them with the assurance that God was on their side (see vv. 7–8).

A city's gates, particularly those of Jerusalem, can also be used figuratively in the Bible to refer to the city's glory, or lack thereof. In Jeremiah 14:2, for example, we read, "Judah mourns,/ And her gates languish;/ They mourn for the land,/ And the cry of Jerusalem has gone up." As we saw earlier in Psalm 87:2, the gates can also refer to the city itself: "The LORD loves the gates of Zion."

Elsewhere in the Bible, gates are used to represent satanic power (see Matt. 16:18), death (see Is. 38:10), righteousness (see Ps. 118:19–20), and salvation (see Matt. 7:13). So we see that gates are an interesting and important part of the biblical story.

The Gates of the Old City

In the Old Testament times, the Jerusalem gates had many different names, both formal and informal. The names of some were old gate, prison gate, Gate of Ephraim, Gate of Benjamin, Gate of Joshua, corner gate, valley gate, gate of the fountain, water gate, king's gate, and high gate. It may very well be that those were not all different gates; some or all of them have been known by more than one name.

The walls and gates of Jerusalem have been destroyed and rebuilt many times in the city's past. The existing walls have eight gates in them allowing movement into and out of the Old City, though one of them is closed off. (The New City is the modern part of Jerusalem built up around the Old City by the Jews since they started immigrating in substantial numbers during the mid-1800s.) Each of those gates is an interesting story in itself, and we want to consider them all in turn.

The first gate we want to look at is the *Dung Gate*. It is on the south side of the city, facing Bethlehem. Its name comes from the fact that in the past, the people of Jerusalem would dump their garbage and refuse out of the city at that gate. It also has an Arabic name that translates "Gate of the Moors."

For many years, the Old City has been divided into Jewish, Armenian, Muslim, and Christian sections. The Dung Gate opens into the Jewish quarter of the Old City. Not far inside it is the Wailing Wall, the only remaining part of the

Jewish Temple and the most revered site in modern Jewish life. The Dung Gate is *the* gate by which people go to and leave that sacred wall, so it is a very busy gate. Many taxis line up just outside to transport the numerous visitors.

The second gate is the *Zion Gate*, also on the south wall but west of the Dung Gate. It gives access to the Armenian quarter of the Old City, and it faces outward to Mount Zion. Just outside this narrow gate is a tomb believed to be King David's, the second most sacred shrine of modern Jews. It is also a revered place for Christians and Muslims. In fact, the Muslim name of the gate translates "Gate of David the Prophet."

The Zion Gate is one of several that had been closed for some time prior to the Israeli capture of the Old City in 1967. It had been kept shut by Jordan, which wanted to limit Jewish access to the Holy City.

The third gate as we go around the city is the *Jaffa Gate*, which is in the western wall and faces toward the city of Jaffa on the Mediterranean coast, some thirty-five miles away. The road to Jaffa starts at this gate, and that road holds two distinctions. In 1870 it became the first street built outside the old city walls; and it is the main road through New Jerusalem, where it is today commonly called the Yafo Road.

Just inside the Jaffa Gate in ancient times stood three of the more important structures in Jerusalem, Herod's palace and citadel and David's tower. The citadel has always been a key point in the many battles for Jerusalem. In the Arab-Israeli struggle for control of the city in 1948, for example, it was the scene of fierce, bloody fighting. The present citadel was built on Crusader foundations by Suleiman the magnificent in 1540.

The Jaffa Gate is the widest of all the gates, one of only a couple that can accommodate both automotive and pedestrian traffic. It is also the gate through which General Allenby entered Jerusalem in 1917. Like the Zion Gate, it was closed by the Jordanians in 1948 and reopened by Israel in 1967.

The Arabs also have a name for this gate that translates "Gate of the Friend." The name relates to the Arabic inscription over the entrance to the gate. The inscription says, "There is no God but Allah and Abraham is his friend."

The fourth gate, in the northwest corner of the Old City, is the *New Gate*. It is in fact relatively new, having been opened in 1889 by the Turkish sultan Abdul-Hamid. Because of its origin, it has an Arabic name that translates "Gate of the Sultan." It opens into the Christian section of the Old City.

The New Gate is yet another that was closed during the Jordanian occupation of the Old City. With the exception of the Dung Gate, which gives access to the Wailing Wall, the gates the Jordanians closed off were on the western side of the Old City. That is where most of Israeli New Jerusalem lies, and that is the reason they were closed.

Our fifth gate is the *Damascus Gate*, on the north side of the city and east of the New Gate. Not surprisingly, it faces toward Damascus, and it gives access to the Muslim section of the Old City. It also faces toward the nearer Jewish towns of Nablus and Shechem, and Israelis often refer to it by one of those two names.

The Damascus Gate is one of the busiest and one of the few that accommodates automotive traffic. It is also picturesque and ornate, and many people think it is the most beautiful gate of them all. It is considered the main gate into the Old City, the proper entrance for visiting crowned heads of state. The swinging metal gates here have many bullet marks in them, constant reminders of the city's violent past and the numerous times it has been fought over.

Built by Suleiman the Magnificent in 1537, the Damascus Gate has two Arabic names that translate "Gate of Victory" and "Gate of the Pillar." That latter name comes from a large pillar that used to stand just outside the gate and can still be seen on some ancient maps of the city. There are many shops that begin just inside the gate, as well as a flight of steps that leads to the top of the city walls.

The sixth gate as we continue clockwise around the city is *Herod's Gate*. Like the Damascus Gate one-half mile to the west, it faces north, opens into the Muslim section of the Old City, and provides access for cars as well as pedestrians. It was sealed shut for many years but reopened by the British in 1917.

The Arabic name for this gate translates "Gate of Flowers." It was at one time called the Sheep Gate, because for many years the weekly sheep market was held just outside it. This name came from the time of Nehemiah. The current name is thought to have been given to the gate by medieval pilgrims who thought the house of Herod Antipas, where Jesus was sent by Pilate, was nearby.

The seventh gate is *Saint Stephen's Gate*. Stephen, the first martyr of the Christian church, was dragged through this gate and stoned just outside for proclaiming the gospel of Jesus Christ. This gate faces east toward the Jordan, and it is only about one-half block north of the Temple area. It also opens into the Muslim section of the city. Through this gate the Israeli army first penetrated the Old City on June 6, 1967, en route to capturing the city and bringing all of it under Israeli control.

The translated Arabic name of this gate is "Saint Mary's Gate." It has also been known as the Lion's Gate because of the reliefs of lions engraved on its facade by the Turks.

The road that continues on into the Old City as you pass through this gate is the beginning of the Via Dolorosa, the traditional route Jesus took from His trial before Pilate to His crucifixion and burial. The traditional site of Pilate's judgment hall, which is also believed to be the site of Herod's great fortress, the Antonia (named after Mark Antony), is on this road but now occupied by a Muslim boys' school.

Finally, the eighth gate, on the east side of the city, is the *Golden Gate*. It is also known as the Eastern Gate, the Beautiful Gate, or, to the Muslims, as the Gate of Mercy. It is the only gate leading from outside the city directly into the Temple area, and it is just a little south of Saint Stephen's Gate. It is also the only one of the eight gates that is still blocked up and not in use today.

The reason the gate is sealed off has to do with one of the many legends about the city's gates, and this gate in particular. The legend in this case is that on the world's final day of judgment, the trumpet of God will sound and the dead will be raised *at this gate*. Believing that legend and hoping to postpone the day of judgment and the end of the world, the Turkish governor of Jerusalem had the gate blocked off in 1530; and so it remains today, more than 450 years later. Jewish tradition says the Messiah will one day enter Jerusalem through this gate. In a similar vein, many Christians believe Jesus, who was and is the promised Messiah, will indeed unblock the gate and enter Jerusalem through it at His second coming (see Ezek. 44:1–3). Another legend says that one of the city's gates leads to hell, and the Golden Gate is the entrance to Paradise. At this time, there is a Muslim cemetery just outside the gate.

The Golden Gate has other significance for Christians as

well. For example, it is believed that Christ made His triumphal entry into Jerusalem at the beginning of His last week through the gate then at this site. Similarly, it is assumed He used it to go out of the city to the Garden of Gethsemane, which is east of the city, on the night when He was betrayed. And it was just inside this gate that Peter and John performed the first miracle of the new church, healing the lame man (see Acts 3:1–10).

We have seen the importance of a city's gates in the ancient Middle East, and certainly the gates of Jerusalem have a most fascinating history. They have witnessed more fighting, in all likelihood, than the gates of any other city on earth. They have seen the comings and goings of proud conquerors and common people through the long centuries. And in silent but clear testament to the power and love of God, they still stand today for all to see. Empires have come and gone, doomed by their abuse of this city, under the judgment of God even as they exulted in their conquests. But the city remains.

8

Jerusalem's Most Precious Places

So much history of great importance to Christians has been made in Jerusalem that it is not surprising that many places precious to our faith are located there. Most of those places have been mentioned in passing as we have looked at Jerusalem in relationship to ancient Israel, Jesus, and the early church. Now we want to look at them a little closer and also see just where they are in the Holy City.

Jerusalem is today a thriving metropolis of about three hundred thousand people, most of whom live in the New City with its broad avenues, modern apartments and office buildings, government chambers, and garden suburbs. Because it has come into being only since the mid-1800s, however, the New City, located south and west of the Old City, is unrelated to biblical history for the most part. Thus, almost all the sites we want to consider are in or just outside the Old City with its narrow, twisting streets and alleys and poor, cramped dwellings.

Places Related to Jesus' Death

It is impossible to list the city's precious places in order of importance, but one site does stand out above all the others. That is Calvary, the place where Jesus paid the price for our sins by being nailed to a cross and hung up to die.

Some scholars feel uncertain of the exact location of Calvary. The Bible only tells us Jesus was taken "to a place called Golgotha, that is to say, Place of a Skull" (Matt. 27:33; only Luke's gospel calls the place Calvary, which is a Latin form of the Hebrew Golgotha, both meaning "skull"). During past centuries Christians generally believed the site to be that of the Church of the Holy Sepulcher in the Christian section of the Old City.

In 1885, however, the famous British general Charles George Gordon, hero of the battle for Khartoum in the Sudan, was walking along the top of the north wall of Jerusalem when he saw a hill just outside the city that looked very much like a human skull. Upon investigation, he came to the conclusion that this was in fact Golgotha. Today, most Protestants accept this site, also known as Gordon's Calvary, as the most likely location of the Lord's crucifixion. A Muslim cemetery now occupies the area, and it is located about a block east of the Damascus Gate.

Most Catholics, on the other hand, still believe the Church of the Holy Sepulcher to be the place where Jesus died. Originally built by the Roman emperor Constantine, this church has several interesting aspects. When Saladin defeated the Crusaders in 1187, he allowed the resident Christians to use the shrine only if the key to the building remained in Muslim hands. The Christians complied, and to this day the key is held by Muslims. Since 1330, it has been held by members of the Nuseibeh family. Also, although since 1958 a "total restoration" of the church has been going on, the building is still in poor repair because the six religious groups who administer it jointly cannot agree on what reconstruction should be done.

Closely associated with Calvary is the tomb of Joseph of Arimathea, in which Jesus was buried. The traditional site, still adhered to by Catholics, Greek Orthodox, Coptics, and others, is also contained within the Church of the Holy Sepulcher. However, as part of his examination of the hill he believed to be Calvary, General Gordon found a Jewish tomb cut out of rock that is immediately west of the crucifixion site, and that is the tomb he and most Protestants have accepted as the burial place of Jesus. When I lead tour groups to Jerusalem, we like to hold a communion service there at the tomb, and it is always one of the spiritual highlights of each trip.

Another precious place just east of the Old City across the Kidron Valley is the Garden of Gethsemane. There, on the night when Jesus was betrayed and arrested, His human nature struggled with the suffering and separation from the Father that were before Him. Being the obedient Son, however, and loving us immeasurably, He accepted the Father's will and bore our deserved punishment for sin.

The present Garden of Gethsemane is maintained by an order of Catholic priests, the Franciscans. It contains eight olive trees that botanists say may be three thousand years old. The historian Josephus says Titus cut down all the trees in and around Jerusalem when he destroyed the city in A.D. 70, so whether these trees somehow escaped the ax or grew later from the roots of leveled trees is not known.

There are two sites in the Garden of Gethsemane that are supposedly the place where Jesus knelt to pray in His night of betrayal. One of these, the Church of All Nations (also known as the Basilica of the Agony), is built over the Rock of Agony, which is the supposed prayer site. The other alleged site of Jesus' prayer is the Grotto of Gethsemane (also known as the Cavern of Agony), which has been kept in its primitive form by the Franciscans since 1392.

The Via Dolorosa, the "Way of Sorrow" or "Way of the

Cross," begins in the Muslim quarter of the Old City and ends in the Christian section. As pilgrims walk this route, they commemorate Jesus' condemnation, mocking, crowning with thorns, scourging, being given His cross to bear to the place of execution, and the execution and burial themselves. It is a solemn journey indeed to walk along and contemplate those things, but thank the Lord it ends with the joyous realization of Jesus' resurrection!

Other Precious Places

The Wailing Wall, mentioned several times previously, is the most sacred part of the city to Jews because it is all that is left of Solomon's Temple. The lower blocks in the wall are from Herod's reconstruction of the Temple, and the higher blocks come from even more recent time periods. Since the actual Temple mount is now occupied by the Dome of the Rock, the Wailing Wall is as close as Jews can get to the former site of the ancient Holy of Holies in the Temple.

The wall's name comes from a variety of sources. Dew covers the wall early in the morning and late at night, and one legend says the dew drops are tears the wall sheds because of Israel's long exile. Another legend says that in the night a white dove, representing the presence of God, appears and coos sadly with the Jews. Yet another reason for the name is that the Jews themselves go to the wall to mourn the loss of the Temple. They also go to present their petitions to God on slips of paper they place in the cracks of the wall. Since Jerusalem came into Jewish hands again in 1967, however, the wall is more often a place of joy rather than sorrow, so the name preferred by Jews today is the Western Wall.

I first visited Jerusalem when it was still under Jordanian control, and in those days houses were built very close to the Western Wall, leaving only a narrow alley between them and the wall. Residents of those houses would throw their garbage out against the wall. After the Israelis captured the city in the Six-Day War, they brought in bulldozers and cleared out those buildings. Today there is a large courtyard in front of the wall that will hold thousands of worshipers at one time. This is also the place to which new soldiers in the Israeli army are brought to take their oath of duty.

The Dome of the Rock and why it is a sacred place to Jew, Muslim, and Christian alike has already been discussed. I would just add here that as the former site of the Temple, this place was visited many times by Jesus. The exact location of many of the other precious places is not clear, as we have seen, so whether Jesus actually visited the places pilgrims go to today is not certain. But there is no doubt whatsoever about the location of the Temple mount and the fact that to walk there is to walk where Jesus walked many times during His earthly life.

Another sacred place just outside the Zion Gate and the south wall of the Old City is the Upper Room, where Jesus held His Last Supper with the disciples and instituted the Communion service. The site pilgrims visit today is again a traditional one, the exact house not known and perhaps no longer even existing.

The church also began in that Upper Room when the Holy Spirit came upon the people gathered there. Thus, it has double significance for Christians.

Interestingly, the Upper Room is in the same building as King David's tomb, which is on the first floor. The site has been marked as David's burial place since about 1173, and the present building was constructed by the Franciscans in 1335. The tomb itself is made of stone and has silver crowns on top of it.

There are two places that can still be visited that go back to the time of Solomon. The first of these is Solomon's stone quarries, also known as the Cave of Zedekiah. These quarries are entered through a small iron gate in the mountain on which the Old City is built, the gate being just north of the Damascus Gate on the north side of the city. From this cave, which extends back into the mountain and under the buildings of the Old City, the stones were cut for the building of Solomon's Temple. The alternate name for these quarries comes from the legend that says Judah's king Zedekiah hid in them during Babylonian King Nebuchadnezzar's siege of the city in 588–78 B.C.

The other site, Solomon's stables, is under the southeast corner of the Temple area. It consists of pillars and arches supporting that part of the Temple platform, and holes in the pillars have been used as stalls for horses in the times of Herod, the Romans, and the Crusaders. Whether they were actually used by Solomon or were ever there in his time is not clear, but doubtful. Up above on this same corner of the Temple area is the "pinnacle" of the Temple, from which Satan tempted Jesus to throw Himself down (see Matt. 4:5–6).

Above the Garden of Gethsemane, east of and across the Kidron Valley from the Old City, is the Mount of Olives, a most precious place. It is the only place outside the city walls from which you can look down into the Old City. As Jesus taught there on several occasions, I'm sure He could see not only the buildings of the city but also the people as they walked and talked, worshiped and did business.

The Mount of Olives is also the place from which the resurrected Lord Jesus ascended into heaven (see Acts 1:9–12). The Church of the Ascension was built some time before A.D. 387 over the site believed to be the place from which He was taken up. In 1187, however, the church was converted to a Muslim mosque, which has remained to this day. The reason for the Muslim interest is that they regard Jesus as a prophet and believe also in His resurrection and ascension, and they believe that on the resurrection day Jesus will raise Muhammad from the dead.

In the last days, when Jesus returns to the earth to fight Antichrist, He will go to the Mount of Olives (many believe He will actually go there first when He comes from heaven), and the mountain will split in half when His feet touch it (see Zech. 14:4).

We could go on and on looking at places of interest and endearment to Christians in Jerusalem, for the city and its immediate environs are full of them. But there is just one last place that I must mention as we close this chapter. When I was living in Jerusalem, and was out walking the streets early one morning as I often did, I found the Old Scotch Church almost by accident. In the yard in front of the church was a large boulder that overlooked the Hinnom Valley, Gehenna, at the foot of Mount Zion on the south side of the city.

I sat down on that boulder and looked at Zion and the valley, then turned and looked at the Temple area and the Mount of Olives to the east. As I was looking around, God spoke to me and gave me the vision that has sparked my ministry ever since. It was there that He told me that if I would obey Him, He would use me to lead one million souls to the Savior. That was truly one of the most precious—and challenging—experiences of my life.

My reason for mentioning the experience here is to say that wherever God speaks to us and meets with us is a precious place. It is wonderful to go to Jerusalem and absorb the history and atmosphere of the place, and it is easy to tune your heart and mind to God there. But God is willing to meet with us anywhere if we will seek His face, so it is not necessary to travel to Israel to be blessed by God. He can speak to us just as clearly in our own living rooms as He spoke to me on that boulder in Jerusalem. May we always seek His face wherever we may be, and then may we obey His calling.

9

Russia's Last Stand at Jerusalem

Russia is a vast land, stretching from the Pacific Ocean and the Orient on one side to the eastern half of Europe on the other side—a land mass almost two-and-a-half times the size of the United States. It is also the most formidable military power in the history of the world, especially when its forces are combined with those of its Soviet bloc allies. We have seen much of what the Bible has to say about Jerusalem, concentrating on the past. Now we want to turn our attention to the future of Jerusalem and Israel, and in that story Russia plays a very large part. (We should also note that Jerusalem often represents symbolically the entire nation of Israel in the Bible.)

Simply put, the Bible says that one day—and I believe it's not too far in the future—Russia will decide to invade Israel, and God will crush its army. Interestingly, leaders in neither country seem to believe that. I have spoken personally to high-level officials in the Israeli government, and none of them will say Russia is going to invade. The Russian leaders, even if they are right now planning the invasion, do not believe the biblical prophecy of their destruction. Regardless, this great empire will surely die at Jerusalem.

The text for these prophecies is Ezekiel 38–39, and it is worth noting that Ezekiel prophesied roughly twenty-five hundred years ago of things that are still in the future. This is further evidence of the divine nature of Scripture. At the same time, Ezekiel's prophecies come with the assurance that everything he foretold will come to pass, because God's Word never fails.

The Ingathering

Our examination of the prophecy of Russia's invasion of Israel begins with the fact that it will take place in "the latter years" (Ezek. 38:8). I believe we are in that time now, the end times, though exactly when things will happen no one can say.

Ezekiel prophesied that after being scattered throughout the earth for centuries, the Jews would be regathered in Israel. Ezekiel 38:8 says, speaking of Russia ("Gog, of the land of Magog," Ezek. 38:2), "In the latter years you will come into the land of those brought back from the sword and gathered from many people." I believe that has already happened.

Looking at the phrase "brought back from the sword," we must remember where the Jews who populated Palestine over the last century came from. They fled massacres, torture, and other forms of persecution in Russia, Eastern Europe, and Arab lands. They came from Germany and other parts of Europe after surviving the horrors and mass murders of Hitler's Holocaust. And once they got to Palestine, the Arabs around them killed as many of them as they could. Since independence in 1948, Israel has never stopped fighting for its life. Truly the regathered nation has been "brought back from the sword."

Turning to the phrase "gathered from many people," we note that the Jews who built the new Israel came from more than one hundred nations in all parts of the world. Out of these many cultures and languages, however, has come one strong nation with its own language, modern Hebrew.

A parallel passage regarding this ingathering of Israel is Jeremiah 31:7–9. Verses 8–9 say, "I will bring . . . the blind and the lame,/ The woman with child/ And the one who labors with child, together;/ A great throng shall return there./ They shall come with weeping." I have met many of the immigrants, and so many of them were pitiful, broken-down people. They had suffered so much that they were still terribly upset and not capable of regular work. Similarly, I have seen them arrive by the boatload at the docks, and often they have been clothed only in tattered rags. They wept—how they wept!— in remembrance of their suffering, but also in joy because they were finally in the Jewish homeland.

Thus we see how the regathering of Israel was in accordance with these prophecies of Ezekiel and Jeremiah, who were contemporaries. And this regathering had to take place before the Russian invasion in the latter days.

Another of the prerequisite fulfillments of prophecy in Ezekiel 38 seems to have taken place, which suggests the invasion could be immediately at hand. Going back to verse 8, it reads, in reference to the new Israel, "all of them dwell safely." A little farther down it says, speaking for Russia, "I will go up against a land of unwalled villages; I will go to a peaceful people, who dwell safely, all of them dwelling without walls, and having neither bars nor gates" (v. 11).

Those passages suggest an Israel that feels secure, very much like the towns and cities of today. Israel feels very secure right now; her farms, villages, and cities "having neither bars nor gates." It is true the towns and kibbutzim of Israel do not have walls like the Old City of Jerusalem. They do have defense, especially near Israel's borders, and they are alert to attack.

The Destruction

The destruction of Russia's invading army will take place in Israel. Scripture such as Revelation 16:16 leads us to believe it will be in the large, fertile, beautiful Plain of Jezreel, some fifty miles northwest of Jerusalem.

The plain is a triangle of about fifteen by fifteen by twenty miles. It is also known as the Plain of Esdraelon, the Plain of Megiddo, or the Valley of Armageddon, and it stretches roughly from Mount Tabor on the north to Mount Gilboa in the south to Mount Carmel in the west.

The Plain of Jezreel is also the world's most famous battleground. Napoleon, great warrior that he was, looked at it and declared it to be the most beautiful battlefield he had ever seen. Egyptians, Hittites, Israelites, Philistines, Assyrians, Syrians, Persians, Greeks, Romans, Crusaders, Turks, British, and more have marched and fought and died on this plain.

For example, Thutmose III, king of Egypt, won a great battle here in 1478 B.C. It was the scene of the victory of Deborah and Barak over Sisera and the Canaanites (see Judg. 4–5). Here Gideon and his three hundred men defeated the Midianites (see Judg. 7). King Josiah of Judah was mortally wounded in combat here (see 2 Chr. 35:20–24), and King Saul and his son Jonathan died near here at Mount Gilboa in a battle with the Philistines (see 1 Sam. 31). And in 1918, the British under General Allenby broke the back of Turkish power in Palestine in a great battle at Megiddo. (For the rest of his life, after being promoted for his conquest of Palestine, Allenby was known as Field Marshall Lord Allenby of Megiddo.)

When the time of Russia's invasion of Israel comes, Ezekiel 38:10 says Russia " 'will make an evil plan.' " Perhaps the Russians will be after the great mineral wealth, including the oil, of the Middle East. Or maybe their goal will be to control Israel as the vital land bridge between three continents. Whatever their reasoning, behind it will be the counsel and prompting of Satan, who has always hated and sought to destroy God's chosen people, Israel, and has hated Jerusalem, the city God loves.

The Bible describes the invasion this way:

> "Then you will come from your place out of the far north, you and many peoples with you, all of them riding on horses, a great company and a mighty army. You will come up against My people Israel like a cloud, to cover the land. It will be in the latter days that I will bring you against My land" (Ezek. 38:15–16).

So Russia will come in great numbers against a land at rest, and God says, " 'My fury will show in My face. For in My jealousy and in the fire of My wrath I have spoken: 'Surely in that day there will be a great earthquake in the land of Israel' " (Ezek. 38:18–19). Russia's arrogance in attacking God's land and people will arouse the wrath of God, who will come to Israel's defense.

In verse 21 God tells us, " 'I will call for a sword against Gog [Russia] throughout all My mountains. . . . Every man's sword will be against his brother.' " Just what that means we can't know for sure, but it may be that God will cause great confusion on the battlefield, with the Russians killing each other.

Ezekiel added:

> " 'The mountains shall be thrown down, the steep places shall fall, and every wall shall fall to the ground. . ' And I will bring him to judgment with pestilence and bloodshed; J will rain down on him, on his troops, and on the many peoples who are with him, flooding rain, great hailstones, fire, and brimstone" (vv. 20,22).

There will be a great flood that will bog down all Russian movement on the plain. Such a thing is not hard to imagine happening there, because the plain was actually a swamp until the early 1920s, when it was drained in a land reclamation project. This time, however, the water will come from a torrential downpour from the hand of God.

There will also be a pestilence of some kind that causes bleeding—very possibly dysentery. And there will be fire and brimstone such as God used to destroy Sodom and Gomorrah in the time of Abraham.

What will be the result of this supernatural attack against the Russian invaders?

> " 'I [God] will turn you [Russia] around and lead you on . . . and bring you against the mountains of Israel, . . . I will give you to birds of prey of every sort and to the beasts of the field to be devoured' " (Ezek. 39:2,4).

What destruction! The birds and other animals will eat the flesh off the dead bodies of the enemy. The passage goes on to say that the people of Israel will continue burning the invaders' weapons in place of firewood for seven years (see 39:9–10), and they will need seven months to bury all the bodies (see 39:12).

We should note also that this defense of Israel will all be

an act of God. The Jews will not lift a finger on this occasion until the conflict is over; and thus all the glory will go to God, as He says in Ezekiel:

> "Thus I will magnify Myself and sanctify Myself, and I will be known in the eyes of many nations. Then they shall know that I am the LORD. . . . So I will make My holy name known in the midst of My people Israel, and I will not let them profane My holy name anymore. Then the nations shall know that I am the LORD, the Holy One in Israel" (38:23; 39:7).

Russia's leaders would do well to heed these verses and look more favorably upon Jerusalem and Israel, and upon their own nearly three million Jews, many of whom would like to go to Israel. Perhaps that way they might even cause the Lord to delay that terrible battle on the plains of northern Israel. But whether they listen or not, the day and the events will come, in God's perfect timing, as He has predicted in Ezekiel.

That battle will be the end of Russia as a threat to Israel and as a world conqueror. However, Russia's defeat will not be the end of Jerusalem's troubles, for after Russia will rise the great Antichrist government and last Gentile world power.

10

Antichrist Rises over the Holy City

The crushing defeat of Russia and its removal from the world scene as a military power sets the stage for the rise of Antichrist, the one who will wage war with the Lord Jesus Christ in the world's climactic Battle of Armageddon. Just where he will come from is not entirely clear, though the Old Testament prophets seem to indicate he will arise out of a revived Roman Empire. Many have speculated he will be the head of the European Common Market, the organization of economic cooperation already in existence there, and that seems to be the most likely explanation.

The early timetable of this figure's career is also not clear, but it seems apparent he will already possess great power at the time of Russia's humiliation. Promising peace and prosperity, many nations will have handed him rule over them very willingly. What is perfectly clear is that he, described as "the beast" in the Revelation, will belong heart and soul to Satan, "the dragon" of the Revelation. We read: "And the dragon gave him his power, his throne, and great authority" (Rev. 13:2). It seems as though the world will also be in awe of the Antichrist because of some sort of miraculous healing he will experience (see Rev. 13:3).

The attack by Russia will give Antichrist the opportunity to occupy Israel under the guise of protecting her from any further attacks, and he will move his headquarters to Jerusalem. Why will he seek out Jerusalem? Like so many before him who have been in the clutches of Satan, he will be drawn to the city with the hope of eventually destroying it and all the Jews. There he will make a pact of peace with the Jews that is supposed to last seven years.

When Antichrist moves into Jerusalem, he will not yet be in total control of the world, and strong forces will move against him from various parts of the earth. We read in Daniel 11:40, "At the time of the end the king of the South shall attack him; and the king of the North shall come against him like a whirlwind, with chariots, horsemen, and with many ships." The result of this conflict will be that Antichrist "shall also enter the Glorious Land, and many countries shall be overthrown" (v. 41). In other words, he will put down those powers and increase his dominion.

He will not stop there, however, for Daniel goes on to say:

> He shall stretch out his hand against the countries, and the land of Egypt shall not escape....But news from the east and the north shall trouble him; therefore he shall go out with great fury to destroy and annihilate many (vv. 42,44).

At that point, he will have become a world dictator. He will have made a reality of the dream of the Caesars, Napoleon, Hitler, and so many others. And he will break his pact with Israel in the middle of the seven years. By that act, this last world emperor will seal his doom.

Economic and Spiritual Oppression

Along with subjugating the world militarily, Antichrist will impose himself upon the world economically and spiritually. He will exert control on even the most routine business transactions, as we read in Revelation 13:16–17:

> And he causes all, both small and great, rich and poor, free and slave, to receive a mark on their right hand or on their foreheads, and that no one may buy or sell except one who has the mark or the name of the beast, or the number of his name.

Those who refuse to receive the mark of the beast will be unable to buy or sell, period—no food, no clothing, nothing.

Antichrist will also reveal his true nature of total opposition to God and demand the worship of the world. Paul described him as "the man of sin ... the son of perdition, who opposes and exalts himself above all that is called God or that is worshiped; so that he sits as God in the temple of God, showing himself that he is God" (2 Thess. 2:3–4).

Apparently the Jewish Temple will have been built in Jerusalem by then, and the vast majority of the world's people will give him and his master the worship they so desire. Revelation 13:4,8 reads:

> So they worshiped the dragon who gave authority to the beast; and they worshiped the beast, saying, "Who is like the beast? Who is able to make war with him?" ... And all who dwell on the earth will worship him, whose names have not been written in the Book of Life of the Lamb slain from the foundation of the world.

There will also be a religious miracle-worker who will come on the scene to promote worship of the Antichrist.

He exercises all the authority of the first beast in his presence, and causes the earth and those who dwell in it to worship the first beast....He performs great signs...And he deceives those who dwell on the earth by those signs which he was granted to do in the sight of the beast (Rev. 13:12–14).

That passage should serve as a warning to us: don't be caught up in miracles. Look for righteousness and holiness in a man's character. When a man is publicized for doing miracles, I want to know the quality of his relationship with his wife and children. I want to know if he pays his bills. True godliness, or lack thereof, shows up in a person's daily living; and there is where we should examine a miracle worker or anyone else who claims to speak or act for God.

Our caution is needed, because as we move into the latter days, demonic spiritual forces are at work as never before. Our Lord Jesus warned us,

"Take heed that no one deceives you. For many will come in My name, saying, 'I am the Christ,' and will deceive many....For false christs and false prophets will arise and show great signs and wonders, so as to deceive, if possible, even the elect" (Matt. 24:4–5,24).

Antichrist will take this worship of himself very seriously, and those of the elect who are not deceived will pay a terrible price for their loyalty to God. We are told in Revelation 13, "And it was granted to him to make war with the saints and to overcome them" (v.7). Further, the second beast who promotes worship of Antichrist "was granted power to...cause as many as would not worship the image of the beast to be killed" (v. 15).

114

ANTICHRIST RISES OVER THE HOLY CITY

Prelude to Armageddon

The hatred of God and His people on the part of Satan and his henchman, Antichrist, will move the world inexorably toward Armageddon. And two further events will frustrate Antichrist and add to his animosity toward God.

First, God will protect 144,000 Jews during this time of the Tribulation to serve some purpose for Him and remain loyal to Him. Many scholars and Bible teachers have surmised that they will be tremendously effective evangelists, for the next verse in Revelation 7 after the discussion of the 144,000 says,

> I looked, and behold, a great multitude which no one could number, of all nations, tribes, peoples, and tongues, standing before the throne and before the Lamb, clothed with white robes....."These are the ones who come out of the great tribulation, and washed their robes and made them white in the blood of the Lamb" (vv. 9,14).

It seems that in spite of intense persecution and mass martyrdom of the saints, a great many people will put their faith in Jesus Christ and have their sins washed away by His atoning blood. It is no wonder, then, that this Antichrist who craves worship will be enraged to see believers in Christ flourishing in spite of his order and persecutions.

Second, Revelation 11 tells us that two supernatural witnesses will rise up for God to denounce Antichrist and proclaim the soon coming of Christ's kingdom on earth.

> And if anyone wants to harm them, fire proceeds from their mouth and devours their enemies....These have power to shut heaven, so that no rain falls in the days of their prophecy; and they have power over waters to turn them to blood, and to

strike the earth with all plagues, as often as they desire (vv. 5-6).

There has been much speculation about the identity of those witnesses, with most of the guesses centering on Moses, Elijah, and Enoch (who, like Elijah, never died but was taken alive into heaven, or "translated"). But regardless of who they will be, the attention they will draw through their miracles and the gospel message they will proclaim will further infuriate Antichrist. They will be miraculously protected by God until they have finished their task, and then "the beast that ascends out of the bottomless pit will make war against them, overcome them, and kill them" (Rev. 11:7). After three and one-half days, however, they will be resurrected by God and will ascend into heaven before their enemies, who will watch in great, and understandable, fear (see Rev. 11:11-12).

The Final Battle

The testimony of the 144,000 Jews and the two witnesses, together with Antichrist's satanic, intense hatred of God and His people, will finally lead him to bring all his forces—the kings of the earth and their armies—to the Middle East to do battle with Christ at Armageddon, the same Plain of Jezreel on which Russia will have been crushed just a few years before (see Rev. 16:16). This decision will show the height of human—and satanic—folly and arrogance.

The apostle John explained what will happen next:

I saw heaven opened, and behold, a white horse. And He who sat on him was called Faithful and True, and in righteousness He judges and makes war....And the armies in heaven,

116

clothed in fine linen, white and clean, followed Him on white horses. Now out of His mouth goes a sharp sword, that with it he should strike the nations....And He has on His robe and on His thigh a name written: KING OF KINGS AND LORD OF LORDS....And I saw the beast, and the kings of the earth, and their armies, gathered together to make war against Him who sat on the horse and against His army (Rev. 19:11,14–16,19).

As we would expect and hope, this opposition of Antichrist to God is useless. We read:

Then the beast was captured, and with him the false prophet who worked signs in his presence, by which he deceived those who received the mark of the beast and those who worshiped his image. These two were cast alive into the lake of fire burning with brimstone. And the rest were killed with the sword which proceeded from the mouth of Him who sat on the horse. And all the birds were filled with their flesh (Rev. 19:20-21).

It will be a tremendous battle, a gory fight, a clash far beyond anything man has ever seen before—but it will also be a very one-sided contest. It isn't a pretty picture the Bible provides, but it allows us to say simply about God's Word and the Tribulation period, "I know how it all ends, and God wins!"

After that great, bloody battle, the Lord Jesus will set up His millennial kingdom on earth, a thousand years of true peace. Then will come the final day of judgment for everyone, and Satan and his followers will be banished to the pit of hell forever.

There is a great deal of controversy in the church today

over the question of whether believers will go through the Tribulation period. My answer, after much study and prayer, is that we will not go through it. Jesus said of that time:

> "But as the days of Noah were, so also will the coming of the Son of Man be. For as in the days before the flood, they were eating and drinking, marrying and giving in marriage, until the day that Noah entered the ark, and did not know until the flood came and took them all away, so also will the coming of the Son of Man be" (Matt. 24:37–39).

Conditions of that time were very much like what we experience today. And Noah, the one believer in God at that point in history, was shut up safely in the ark by God. Similarly, our world today is every bit as wicked and debauched as were Sodom and Gomorrah; and Lot, the one believer in God in those cities, was spared from the Lord's destruction of them. In like manner, I believe, the Lord will spare us who believe in Jesus Christ from the great Tribulation at the end of this age. But we must first be certain our lives are bound up with Christ's life and our sins have been washed away in His sinless blood.

If we have that certainty, we need never fear the end times and the tremendous destruction that will be wrought on the earth when the last two great empires to oppose God—Russia and Antichrist—will be crushed after they move against Jerusalem and its people.

11

Will America Die at Jerusalem?

We have seen what will happen in the end times to Russia and Antichrist because of their opposition to God and their determination to conquer Jerusalem and all of Israel. But did you notice as we were looking at the biblical passages describing those events that there was no reference to any nation or power we could identify as the United States? Isn't that strange, given that we are entering the end times and America is one of the world's two superpowers? Isn't the United States the most powerful and loyal ally of Israel?

The events of the end times as described in the Bible are ordained by God, and there can be no doubt but that things will occur as He has foretold. The absence of any mention of a nation we could say is the United States, therefore, is a cause for great distress among those of us who live in and love this nation. Where will America be at that time?

The conclusion we must draw is very sad and sobering, and it should serve as a loud warning to our beloved United States. Simply put, the United States will no longer be a world power in the end times. It will not be a significant enough nation to play a major role in the events of those days—that is the most obvious answer.

What would lead to the waning of our power? I am afraid the process is already far advanced, because we are no longer a nation under God. We are moving steadily away from Him and His purposes and blessing. Materialism, sexual sin, pride, deceit, hypocrisy, and a host of other sins are all rampant in America today; and unless we begin again to seek the Lord, I see us racing rapidly toward moral dissolution.

Another danger for America, and more to the point for this study, is that I am afraid our national support for Israel is weakening, and that would be disastrous. We have looked at how Jerusalem is a golden bowl full of vipers, how it has served as a center for the great spiritual conflict going on in our world. Those who hate God hate Jerusalem and its people, and those who love Him love the city and its inhabitants.

The Babylonian Empire died on the night that its king stooped to the grossest mockery of God. Similarly, I believe the real collapse of the British Empire began in this century with its mistreatment of the Jews and its mishandling of Palestine starting at the end of World War I. When I began my ministry and shortly thereafter toured the world with Howard Carter, Great Britain was still a major global empire. That was in the 1930s and Britannia still ruled the waves. It controlled nations all over the earth. But its decline began about that same time, when it was favoring the Arabs over Israel. By 1948, when British forces left Palestine, England's empire was waning. And the same fate of fading to a second-rate power could await America if our support of Israel does not remain strong.

We would do well to look again at a few verses from the Bible first quoted in chapter 1. Psalm 46:5 says of Jerusalem, "God is in the midst of her;/ she shall not be moved;/ God shall help her,/ just at the break of dawn." In Zechariah 1:14 God said, "I am zealous for Jerusalem/ And for Zion with great zeal." In Psalm 129:5 we read, "Let all those who hate Zion/ Be put to shame and turned back." In contrast to that, the inspired writer of Psalm 122:6 said of Jerusalem, "May they prosper who love you."

The message is clear: Despite the many failings of the Israeli people in their city of Jerusalem, God has chosen them and determined to bless them. Accordingly, He will also bless those who bless Israel, but He will bring low those who would harm the Jews.

In the past, America's support of Israel had been strong and sure. Beginning in 1956, however, that changed. In the Sinai War of that year, when my family and I were living in Jerusalem, France and England had an agreement with Israel. They would take the Suez Canal from Egypt, and Israel would fight across the Sinai desert to meet them.

President Eisenhower of the United States, however, was determined that would not happen. He forced France and England to withdraw from the conflict, threatening to fight on the side of Egypt; and he also cut off all American supplies to Israel—food, medicine, oil, and everything else. If France had not provided those essentials, my family and the rest of the people in Israel would have been in dire straits. Believe me, we were very grateful to France for standing by Israel.

What has become of the United States since 1956? Note carefully. We have lost the last two wars we have fought, in Korea and Vietnam. Our society has begun to fall apart rapidly. Violent rebellion broke out on our college campuses. The drug problem, sexual sin, and divorce have exploded. Our economy has become far less stable and far more vulnerable to foreign competition.

All these things may seem unrelated on the surface, but that is not the case. It is not a coincidence that these problems erupted after our desertion of Israel in 1956. And this

121

turning away, however gradual, has continued in recent years as we have sought to please Arab oil sheikhs. Thus, like Babylon, Persia, Rome, and all the others, America has put its hand into the golden bowl of Jerusalem and is in imminent danger of being put on the shelf by God, so to speak, as a world power.

It is not too late for the United States to once again become a Christian nation, and for us to renew our commitment to Israel. I believe the Lord would honor such a commitment and continue to bless us with strength and prosperity.

Conversely, if there is no such revival and renewed commitment to Israel, I can see the moral degradation of our day growing ever more widespread and severe, and the United States decaying from within, as did Rome and many other great empires of the past. Perhaps then Russia could force us to our knees.

Therefore, it is essential that those of us who love the Lord and this wonderful democracy pray fervently and also make our voices heard. I have sent telegrams to all of our presidents and other elected officials, to remind them of the importance of our support for Israel. I am not personally responsible for the decisions of our leaders, but I am responsible for giving them the truth of God's Word and supporting them in prayer.

Everyone who can should visit Jerusalem at least once. It is an incomparable city chosen by God, and to walk its streets is to partake of a richer history than that of any other city on earth. I can't help feeling especially close to God every time I go there.

Above all else, however, we should seek the Lord wherever we are, and we should pray and work for the safety of

WILL AMERICA DIE AT JERUSALEM?

God's chosen city and people.

Jerusalem: A Chronology of Events

c.996 B.C.   David conquers the Jebusite city.

c.880 B.C.   King Jehoash of Israel defeats the army of Judah and sacks the city.

c.700 B.C.   Assyria under King Sennacherib attacks the city but is driven away by God.

c.605 B.C.   Nebuchadnezzar of Babylon captures the city.

586 B.C.   Babylon destroys the city because of the revolt of Zedekiah.

539 B.C.   Persia under Cyrus the Great takes control of the city after overthrowing Babylon.

516 B.C.   Temple reconstruction completed under Zerubbabel.

445 B.C.   The entire city is rebuilt by Nehemiah, cupbearer to Persia's King Artaxerxes.

330 B.C.   Control of the city passes to Greece, as Alexander the Great brings an end to the Persian Empire.

323 B.C.   Egypt takes control when Alexander's empire is divided after his death.

198 B.C.   The Seleucid (Syrian) Empire takes the city from Egypt.

165 B.C.   In revolt against the abominations of Antiochus Epiphanes, the Maccabees defeat Syria and capture the city.

63 B.C.   The Roman Empire extends its reach to Judea when its general, Pompey the Great, takes the city from the Hasmonaeans.

A.D. 70	The Roman general Titus destroys the city as part of Rome's campaign to crush the revolt of the Zealots.
135	In response to another Jewish revolt, Roman emperor Hadrian makes the city pagan and forbids Jews to enter it on pain of death.
313	The Roman emperor Constantine I makes Christianity the official religion of the empire and Jerusalem a Christian city.
438	Jews finally allowed back into the city by Rome.
637	An Arabic Muslim army invades Palestine and conquers the city under the caliph Omar I.
687-91	The Muslim Dome of the Rock is built over the site of the Jewish Temple.
1099	The European Crusaders capture the city, defeating its Turkish Muslim masters.
1186	Muslims retake the city and remove all signs of the Crusader occupation.
1517	All of Palestine is won by Sultan Selim I of Turkey's Ottoman Empire.
1917	British and allied troops take the city without firing a shot at the end of World War I under General Allenby.
1922	The League of Nations puts Palestine under a British protectorate.
1948	Having been approved by the United Nations, the existence of the modern state of Israel is formally declared in a speech by David Ben-Gurion, but Jerusalem remains under international control.
1950	Jerusalem is made the capital of Israel, although Jordan continues to control the Old City.
June 1967	Israel recaptures the Old City in the Six-Day War, making Jerusalem a unified city under Jewish control for the first time in more than two thousand years.